The SEBAGO LAKES REGION

A BRIEF HISTORY

NED ALLEN

THE History PRESS

Published by The History Press
Charleston, SC 29403
www.historypress.net

First published 2013

Manufactured in the United States

ISBN 978.1.60949.146.8

Library of Congress CIP data applied for.

CONTENTS

INTRODUCTION

This book is about the Sebago Lakes Region in western Maine, which is not a neatly defined region, either geographically or culturally. No doubt some readers may feel that I have included towns that don't belong or didn't include ones that do. The region certainly consists of more than the area served by the Lake Region School District, which serves the towns of Bridgton, Naples, Sebago and Casco. Using a definition that includes those towns that directly border Sebago Lake—Naples, Sebago, Casco, Raymond, Windham and Standish—expands the region but leaves out Bridgton, one of the larger towns in the area and traditionally a commercial and industrial center serving many of the surrounding communities.

If we also include the towns along the shores of Long Lake, which connects to Sebago through Brandy Pond and the Songo River, we have a region that includes Bridgton and Harrison as well as the six towns listed above. There is a compelling argument for this definition, since the Presumpscot River flows out of the southern end of Sebago Lake into Casco Bay in Portland Harbor. This was the primary means of transportation into the region for the Native Americans who inhabited the land for thousands of years and for European emigrants up until the arrival of the railroad in the second half of the nineteenth century. The Cumberland and Oxford Canal, which opened in 1830, upgraded this connection to the sea, creating a shorter and more navigable waterway that emptied into the Fore River and Portland Harbor. The total distance from Harrison to Portland following this route is approximately fifty miles.

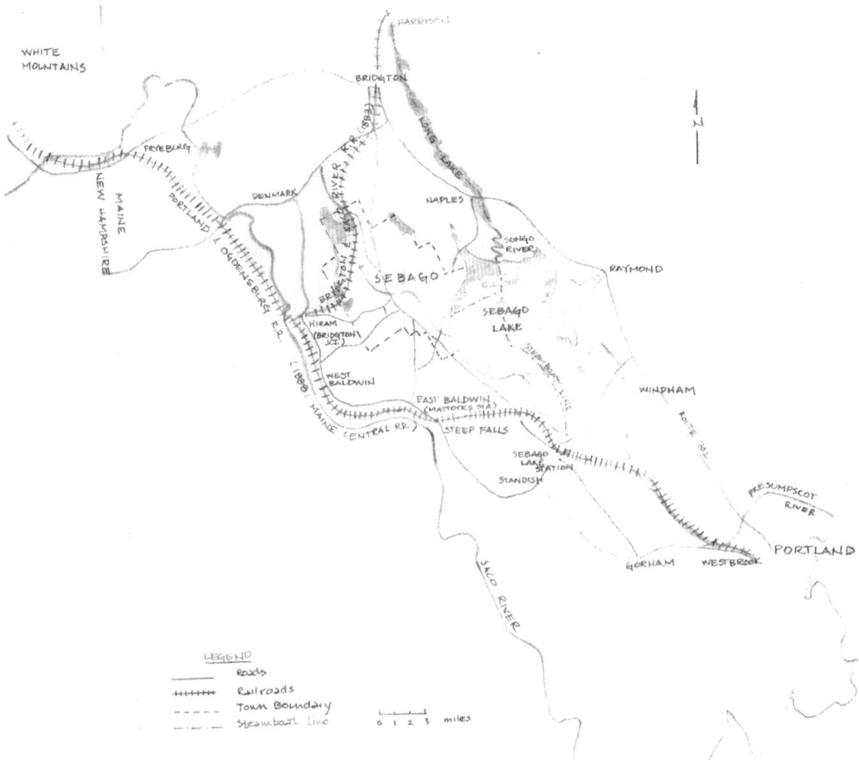

This map shows the major transportation routes connecting the Sebago-Long Lake Region to the world. *Map by Carol Colby, 1992.*

With the core of communities stretching from Standish and Windham at the southern end of Sebago Lake to Harrison at the northern tip of Long Lake, we begin to establish a meaningful definition of the region. But like so much of life, it's not quite that simple. For one thing, town boundaries have changed considerably through the years. Otisfield, for example, was originally much larger than it is today. In 1805, Otisfield's land east of Long Lake and West of Crooked River was set off to form the town of Harrison. In 1834, Otisfield lost even more of its territory to Naples, which was created from portions of Raymond, Harrison, Sebago and Bridgton, as well as Otisfield. To further complicate the picture, in 1978, Otisfield, not wishing to be taxed for the construction of the Cumberland County Civic Center in Portland, seceded from Cumberland County and joined Oxford County, and Otisfield today does not border any of the waterways described above.

Similarly, in 1826, the town of Sebago was carved out of the northern half of Baldwin, which also does not directly border these waterways today. An argument could also be made for excluding Hiram, which is on the Saco River west of Sebago. But in 1882, the narrow-gauge Bridgton and Saco River Railroad was built connecting to the standard-gauge Maine Central in Hiram, with its terminus in Bridgton, later extended to Harrison. For over forty years, this little rail line played as important a role for the region as the canal had for an earlier generation. Arguably, parts of other towns—the southern portion of Windham, for example, and western portions of Standish—may not seem to some to be quite in the "Lakes Region," but more in the orbit of Gorham and Westbrook, whose proximity to Portland has profoundly influenced their development, particularly in the twentieth century.

All of this means that we will have to be content with a somewhat vaguely-defined concept of the Lakes Region, encompassing, at its heart, at least parts of Standish, Windham, Raymond, Casco, Naples, Sebago, Bridgton, Harrison and Otisfield. Other towns, such as Hiram and Denmark, are also part of the story. Adding to the confusion, today there are two chambers of commerce that serve the region: the Sebago Lakes Region Chamber of Commerce and the Greater Bridgton Lakes Region Chamber of Commerce. Several towns are members of both chambers, and they both include towns that are not specifically covered in this book. While all of these towns have much in common, and there are solid reasons for them to be working cooperatively together, this book focuses primarily on the nine towns listed above. Other towns that are in one of these two chambers, and which therefore can claim to be part of the region, include Gray, New Gloucester, Fryeburg, Lovell, Stow, Sweden, Waterford, Limington, Limerick and Brownfield. In fact, Gorham, which is in neither chamber, should not be ignored, since it shares the Presumpscot River and important water power sites with Windham.

Perhaps it is for the best that we are not adhering to an area strictly delineated by political boundaries. While we must turn to town histories and other sources that are defined by official political boundaries for information, one of the primary aims of this book is not to produce a compilation of individual town histories, but to paint a picture of the development of the Lakes Region as a whole. It should be noted that in order to maintain consistency, discussions of population figures and demography, which shed important light on the story of the Lakes Region, will include, and be restricted to, the following municipal entities (and their predecessors): Baldwin (because it once included what is now the town of Sebago),

The view of Sebago Lake from the tower on top of Douglas Mountain in 2012. *Photo by the author.*

Bridgton, Casco, Denmark, Harrison, Hiram, Naples, Otisfield, Raymond, Sebago, Standish and Windham. Also, this is a brief history, not a scholarly tome, and it relies heavily on secondary sources. I am indebted to all those who have written about the region's history in the recent and not-so-recent past, and I have tried to give credit where credit is due.

The 1,400-foot summit of Douglas Mountain in Sebago, the highest point in Cumberland County, affords a panoramic view of much of the rugged, hilly landscape of the Lakes Region. On a clear day, standing atop the stone tower built on this hilltop in 1925, the city of Portland and Casco Bay, about thirty miles away, are visible on the southeast horizon. To the north and west, a dramatic panorama unfolds, encompassing the hills and mountains of western Maine and the White Mountains of New Hampshire. Closer by, Sebago Lake and a number of smaller ponds are framed by wooded hillsides, punctuated here and there by an outcropping of ledge. Occasionally, a clearing with an isolated house or a small cluster of buildings can be spotted. Across the valley at the base of Peaked Mountain, the Northwest River winds through a large cleared area. But this clearing is not fertile farmland surrounding a river, but a bog, accessible primarily by canoe or kayak when not frozen.

Before 1900, the view from the top of Douglas Mountain would have been very different. Open fields led to a few farmhouses lower down the slope. Beyond, while there was no dearth of woodland, there was far less forest than today. Cleared hillsides, geometrically crisscrossed with stone walls, were dotted with farms. On the far side of the Northwest River, instead of unbroken forest, there were about a dozen farmsteads, four of them high up the side of the mountain. This small community of a dozen or so homesteads was known as "the Folly." By the second half of the twentieth century, it was visible only as a series of abandoned cellar holes and an old cemetery in the woods.

Perhaps the best illustration of the open landscape of that era can be seen in a comparison between two sets of photographs, taken at least seventy-five years apart, from the top of the hill behind the Oliver Pike House in Sebago, on a shoulder of Douglas Mountain. Both show two ponds, Southeast Pond on the left and Barker Pond toward the center, nestled among a series of hills. In one of the photographs, taken in December 1990, only a small area in the immediate foreground (clear-cut in 1988 to open up the view) and two fairly small areas on more distant hillsides are open fields. The rest is heavily forested. The other photographs date from no later than 1915, probably earlier. In these pictures, most of the middle foreground is open fields, strewn with boulders, punctuated by occasional large trees and crisscrossed by stone walls. On close inspection, roads, buildings and occasionally details such as

A view from the hill behind the Pike farm in Sebago, probably circa 1910. *Collection of the author.*

A second view, overlapping the previous view, from the hill behind the Pike farm in Sebago. *Collection of the author.*

A panoramic view from the same spot in Sebago, taken in 1991. *Collection of the author.*

the orderly furrows of small plots of cropland are visible. The fairly small areas that are open fields in the later photograph are much larger in the earlier ones. Between one-third and one-half of the closer hillsides, where detail is distinguishable, are open in the older photograph.

Although the landscape was far more open in late nineteenth-century Sebago than it is today, it was already reverting to woodland at that time.

In New England, generally, the amount of land cleared for farming peaked around 1880, but in the town of Sebago, farmland was already shrinking dramatically. According to the Agricultural Census taken in 1870, approximately 6,800 of the 12,900 acres of agricultural land in Sebago were classified as woodland, or just over 50 percent. By 1880, that figure had risen to nearly 9,700, an astonishing increase of over 40 percent.

Sebago Lake, whose name is Abenaki for "Great stretch of water," is Maine's second-largest lake. It is approximately eight miles across at its widest point and ten miles long, with a surface area of over forty-seven square miles, and at 316 feet, it is Maine's deepest lake. It is within a three-hour drive from Boston and an hour or so from Portland, Maine's largest city, making it a popular destination for day trips as well as longer vacations. It is estimated that the summer population is two to four times greater than the year-round population. There are numerous second homes in the region, and many families have been coming back to the same place each summer for generations. The waterway that was once the region's lifeblood as a means of transportation and an important artery for importing and exporting goods remains one of its great resources, but now as a recreational area, enjoyed by local residents and visited by thousands of people each year. Countless smaller lakes and ponds also draw people for fishing, swimming and other watersports, while the scenic and hilly terrain provides opportunities for hiking, bicycling, both cross-country and downhill skiing, snowboarding, snowmobiling and other off-road motorsports, hunting, golfing and attending cultural events and festivals.

Its proximity to Portland and the Lewiston-Auburn metropolitan area also makes it something of a bedroom community, with many residents commuting as much as an hour or more to work each day. Between 1970 and 2000, the population in the towns included in this study more than doubled, from over 21,000 to slightly more than 49,000, an increase of over 130 percent. This far outstripped both Maine's overall population growth, which rose from around 977,000 to nearly 1.25 million, an increase of about 28 percent, and the United States' population growth, which rose from 203 million to 281 million, a roughly 38 percent increase, during the same period. The suburban sprawl that was a hallmark of the post–World War II years was most evident in North Windham, where Route 302, the (Theodore) Roosevelt Highway, is lined with shopping centers, fast-food restaurants, national chain and "big box" stores. Standish and Bridgton have also witnessed some of this type of development, with shopping centers that include a major

Population Trends of the Sebago Lakes Region

	Lakes Region*		State of Maine		United States	
Year	**Population**	**% Change**	**Population**	**% Change**	**Population**	**% Change**
1790	2,808		96,540		3,929,214	
1820	10,468	+273%	298,335	+209%	9,638,453	+145%
1850	17,637	+68%	583,169	+95%	23,191,876	+141%
1880	16,639	-6%	648,935	+11%	49,371,340	+113%
1910	12,819	-23%	742,731	+14%	92,228,496	+87%
1940	13,032	+2%	847,226	+14%	132,164,569	+43%
1970	23.009	+77%	977,260	+15%	203,211,926	+54%
2000	56,258	+145%	1,274,923	+30%	281,421,906	+38%

*For the purposes of this analysis, and as discussed elsewhere in the text, the Sebago Lakes Region is defined as comprising the towns of Baldwin, Bridgton, Casco, Denmark, Harrison, Hiram, Naples, Otisfield, Raymond, Standish, and Windham. Population figures derived from U.S. Census Returns.

Chart of population growth in Sebago Lakes Region, State of Maine and United States, 1790–2000, at thirty-year intervals.

grocery chain and fast food franchises. Elsewhere, subdivisions made up of ranch houses and other familiar twentieth-century architectural forms have appeared, in some cases opening up steep hilltop sites, occasionally with exclusive gated communities.

Still, there are many people living in the Lakes Region today whose families have lived here for many generations; sometimes they can trace their ancestry back to the earliest settlers. Bean suppers and other community events bring people together and raise money for a wide array of worthy causes, and in times of need, neighbors know that they have each other to help get them through.

Chapter 1

TAMING THE WILDERNESS

Native Americans and Early European Settlement

PREHISTORIC SEBAGO AND INDIGENOUS PEOPLES

Archaeologists tell us that the Sebago Lakes Region has been inhabited by human beings for as many as eleven thousand years, when the glacier that once covered the region receded and plant and animal species moved in. However, our picture of the Native Americans who lived in the Sebago Lakes Region prior to their first contact with Europeans is a somewhat muddy one. Accounts of the indigenous peoples of New England from early European explorers, though informative, reflect the cultural prejudices of the time. Often described as "savages," they were viewed as uncivilized and inferior. Additionally, Europeans brought infectious diseases, particularly smallpox, to the shores of North America, where they were previously unknown. Lacking any resistance to the germs, an estimated 75 to 90 percent of the New England Indians were wiped out in the early to mid-1600s. This meant that many inland tribes were decimated before they had much direct contact with white men, and since their history was based on an oral tradition, much of their own story was lost.

Fishing was almost certainly an important aspect of life for the people who lived around the lake. Geologists speculate that at one time, Atlantic salmon, shad and alewives made it past the falls of the Presumpscot River to spawn in Sebago Lake. The American eel, on the other hand, may have moved in the opposite direction, maturing in the lake and moving downriver into the Atlantic to spawn. "Land-locked" salmon and other species, of course, were in the lake year-round. Scientists have suggested that salmon became "trapped" in the lake thousands of years ago, when the water level dropped to a point that is lower than today. Being creatures of habit, even after water levels rose high enough for them to again head out to sea, they stayed in the familiar waters of the lake. Lake dwelling salmon in Maine are also found in Sebec Lake, West Grand Lake and Green Lake. They rarely exceeded five pounds in these other lakes, but in the open waters of Sebago, where they could feed on large schools of rainbow smelt, they often grew to over three feet in length, weighing over twenty pounds.

Although the lake had taken its basic shape and structure by the time the first human inhabitants moved into the area, changing climatic and geologic conditions affected the fish, game and edible plants that were available. The first vegetation to take root following the retreat of the glacier that covered the area until about thirteen thousand years ago created a tundra-like environment with grasses and shrubs. Forests appeared as the environment warmed, although their composition altered with changing conditions. The forests that the first Europeans encountered formed only about one thousand years ago, although the animal species of ten thousand years ago are pretty much the same as those we find today. Deer and moose were present (deer more than moose), as were caribou at times. Waterfowl, amphibians and reptiles, especially turtles, are also thought to have been part of the Native American diet.

While the specific details of pre-contact Native American life in the Sebago Lakes region are not readily available, the general outlines of their life in Maine are. Maine was first colonized by humans that archaeologists have termed "Paleo-Indians" at the end of the last ice age, roughly ten thousand to eleven thousand years ago. The Sebago area residents of the next period, the Archaic, inhabited the region from roughly ten thousand to three thousand years ago. They adopted a less nomadic lifestyle than that of their Paleo-Indian predecessors, moving seasonally from place to place within a defined territory, going where the environment and resources were optimal for whatever time of year it was. The introduction of ceramics about three thousand years ago marked the beginning of the third period, known, appropriately enough, as the Ceramic Period. Population increased during this time (until the arrival of Europeans), and the lifestyle became less nomadic.

Artifacts from prehistoric peoples have been found in abundance along the shores of Sebago Lake for centuries, attesting to the presence of these peoples in many sites around the lake and its connected waterways. Farmers and others turned up artifacts while plowing fields or otherwise going about their daily business, and by the end of the nineteenth century, collectors were actively seeking them. "Relicking" even became a verb, meaning to search for Indian relics. While these activities would certainly not live up to the standards of modern archaeological practice, several large collections were amassed. In some cases, the collectors took pains to catalog the artifacts and document where they were found, and they have since made their way into the collections of statewide and local museums and historical societies.

The tribes in the Sebago Lakes Region were Abenaki, part of the larger Wabanaki confederacy. Confusingly, "Wabanaki" and "Abenaki" are actually different variations of the same word, which is generally accepted to mean "People of the Dawnland." However, the term "Wabanaki" usually refers to a larger group, which includes the Abenaki, who lived in much of what is now northern New England, from Maine to northern Vermont. This group included the Passamaquoddy, Malecite and Mi'kmaq, Cowasuck and Sokoki tribes. In recent times, some commentators have referred to them as the "Invisible People" whose identity, language, history and culture are hidden from sight. Many moved to Canada during the 1700s, but descendants of these first residents of the region point out that others stayed in Maine, their native homeland, or later returned. They found ways to survive, hiding their identity "in plain sight," as anthropologist Margaret Bruchac put it.

In recent years, scholars have adopted a more even-handed perspective on the study of Native Americans than did earlier generations. These early interpretations, based almost solely on written, Anglo-European sources, have been replaced and augmented with a more balanced and diversified approach. Today, scholars apply a more critical analysis of the early European accounts, and archaeological investigations have helped to flesh out the story. Additionally, Native American voices have been asserting their own interpretations more aggressively, in publications and on websites that present their perspective and encourage further study. The Nedoba website (http://www.nedoba.org/) puts the case succinctly:

> *As Abenaki descendants speak out, our vision is improved. However, there is still much work to be done before the picture becomes clear. Modern scholars are rediscovering the Abenaki people throughout the Northeast. This is being accomplished by combining French, English, and Dutch documents with personal diaries, captivity stories, family genealogies, and oral tradition. The Abenaki story is a giant jigsaw puzzle with most of its pieces scattered by the winds of time. By gathering existing documented information, we*

begin to make sense of the pieces we have. By researching family histories, we find missing pieces. By digging through old reports, ledgers, and journals, we find pieces we were not aware existed. By putting these pieces together, we begin to understand the role the Abenaki people played in the history of the Northeast and the methods they used to survive to the present.

The Abenaki lived in small bands, led by a chief who served as a sort of advisor or facilitator for the group, which relied on consensus-based decision making. There was often a separate chief for war. Both men and women were involved in councils that decided matters relating to war, while smaller groups representing each family dealt with other important questions. They fished and hunted, building traps to capture game, as well as using the bow and arrow. They also grew corn, beans and squash, most intensely in southern areas, and gathered berries, nuts, mushrooms and medicinal plants, as well as making maple syrup. Their dwellings, known as wickiups, were covered in birch bark, as were the canoes they built. Not surprisingly, they relied heavily on waterways for transportation. In fact, the vast majority (over 90 percent) of the prehistoric archaeological sites in Maine are located adjacent to canoe-navigable waters, whether they be by the seacoast, a lake, river, stream, swamp or a former shoreline.

The Pequawkets, who are most closely associated with the area around Fryeburg, apparently maintained summer settlements along the western shore of Highland Lake in Bridgton, which the early white settlers called Crotched Pond (the name was changed in the late nineteenth century, to be more congenial to the summer visitors who were starting to frequent the area). By 1768, when the town was first being surveyed to set out the individual lots for settlement, there was little evidence of the Indians' presence in the area, although Solomon Wood, the surveyor, did report seeing an "Indian dog" in the area that is now downtown Bridgton. Bridgton was apparently traversed by heavily used Indian trails (much as Route 302 is heavily used today), and the Native Americans who used them were reputed to have been friendly, often trading at the store that Benjamin Kimball, the town's first settler, established on the shore of Long Lake. An Englishman, Major Winthrop Hilton, who led a scouting party in 1703, described what he termed a fort in what is today Fryeburg. There were about one hundred wigwams inside a circular palisade (vertical posts in the ground), with occasional openings, or gates of some sort. This was the village of Pequaweket, or Pigwacket, as it is sometimes termed.

Near this village, a skirmish known as the "Battle of Lovewell's Pond" took place in 1725. Captain John Lovewell, from Nashua, New Hampshire, was commanding a small band of men who had set out to suppress the Indians and collect bounties that had been set on their scalps. Both sides suffered heavy casualties, including both Lovewell and the Pequawket chief, Paugus. Although in military terms it is hard to say which side won, this incident (some historians feel it should be more appropriately termed a "fight" than a battle) was seen as a turning point in the ongoing hostilities between the English and the Native Americans of western Maine. It was celebrated throughout northern New England, and a century later, Henry Wadsworth Longfellow, Henry David Thoreau and Nathaniel Hawthorne (who spent a portion of his childhood in Raymond) all wrote accounts of it. In 1904, the Society of Colonial Wars in the Commonwealth of Massachusetts erected a granite marker in the woods to commemorate the event.

Around 1780, settlers in Baldwin (then part of Flintstown Plantation) apparently found Indians living near Ingalls' Pond and the falls. Other evidence of Indian occupation could be found on Frye Island, the largest island on Sebago Lake. It is separated from the mainland by a narrow passage known as "The Gut." A cliff, known as "Frye's Leap" or "The Images," was decorated with pictographs, now faded beyond restoration, painted by Native Americans. The name "Frye's Leap" derives from a legendary incident when Indian hunter Captain Frye, from Scarborough, was being pursued by a band of Indians. He leaped from the eighty-foot cliff onto the frozen, snow-covered lake and thus escaped his pursuers. When steamboat

An old postcard of Frye's Leap on Sebago Lake. The Indian pictographs known as "The Images" are now only faintly distinguishable. *Collection of the author.*

excursions became popular in the late nineteenth and early twentieth centuries, a figure dressed as an Indian would appear, brandishing a rifle and making stereotypical war cries.

Another legend about this famous rock has a decidedly unhappy ending. It involves an Abenaki girl who was apparently the subject of one of these pictographs. According to Herbert G. Jones in *Sebago Lake Land*, the girl was named Naragora, the daughter of Waldola, an old hunter. She was betrothed to a young chief who had gone to the wars at Quebec. A young white man, sick, wounded and starving, arrived at the wigwam. Naragora watched over him and nursed him back to health. One day when her father was away hunting, the white man asked her to marry him, persistently repeating his proposal many times. Her answer was always no. Finally, out of frustration, she told him that she was to marry a young man of her tribe and that he would return in three months. This enraged the white man, who threatened her, and she fled to her father. When they returned, the white man was gone. However, a few weeks later, she was kidnapped by the man. He took her away into the forest, but that night, while he slept, she escaped and the next day was back with Waldola, her father. He felt they needed to leave the vicinity of the lake, but a group of white men appeared as they were preparing to flee. A struggle ensued, and Waldola was shot and killed. Naragora was determined not to be captured. She ran but was unable to outrun her pursuers. They caught up to her on top of the cliff, and she jumped to her death to escape.

THE ARRIVAL OF EUROPEANS

Of course, the white men's incursions into the region took place under the auspices of the Commonwealth of Massachusetts, since Maine was part of Massachusetts until 1820 (when it was granted statehood as part of the Missouri Compromise). Most of the towns in the Lake Region were created by grants from the Massachusetts General Court, as the legislature was known. The grants originated as payment for military services rendered, either in the wars with the French and Indians in the first half of the eighteenth century or in the American Revolution.

For much of the 1700s, the Massachusetts colony claimed a large portion of what would eventually become southern New Hampshire. The result of this was that both Massachusetts and New Hampshire made land grants in this area, leading to confusion and conflict. In 1741, this dispute was finally resolved by the English government in favor of New Hampshire, an action that effectively nullified a number of previous grants by Massachusetts. Many of the towns in the Sebago Lakes Region were created by grants to individuals (or perhaps more commonly, to their heirs), known as the proprietors, in place of these original grants.

The proprietors themselves rarely moved to the new settlements, which were known as plantations prior to incorporation as townships. The term "plantation" as applied in seventeenth- and eighteenth-century New England was clearly used in the English sense, which, according to *Black's Law Dictionary*, referred to "an original settlement in a new country," rather than the more familiar meaning of "a large cultivated estate," generally associated with the American south. At any rate, the proprietors' goal in establishing settlers on their land grants was to profit from rising land values as the wilderness was turned into a settled landscape. Typically, they were required to settle a certain number of homesteads in a given period of time and provide a minister, a meetinghouse and a school for the settlers.

This painting by John Mead II depicts the area in what is now North Bridgton where Jacob Kimball, Bridgton's first settler, built his house and opened a store. *Courtesy Bridgton Historical Society.*

Map of Windham, from *Atlas of Cumberland Co. Maine,* F.W. Beers & Co., New York, 1871.

Often the first grants the proprietors themselves made to the settlers who actually moved to the new community contained strategic incentives to encourage the creation of essential infrastructure. In Bridgton, for example, Jacob Kimball was awarded a lot near the northern end of Long Lake in exchange for operating a store and providing boat service from Pearsontown (now Standish) at the southern end of Sebago Lake. Typically the proprietors would grant land and water rights on a promising river or stream in exchange for an agreement by the grantee to build a sawmill or gristmill and operate it for a certain number of years. In Otisfield, for example, George Pierce established his homestead at Edes Falls (now part of Naples), partly because of the available water power and partly because it provided easy access to the major waterway via the Crooked River. One of Pierce's conditions was use of the proprietors' boat.

The first European settlement in the district was in the town of Windham, logically enough, since it sits at the mouth of the Presumpscot River, which, at a time when roads were a rough track through the woods at best, was the major thoroughfare to the coast. Most of the first wave of white men who came to the region were loggers, cutting wood, often huge white pine trees destined to be used as masts for the Royal Navy. Once cut, these massive logs were taken to the "Royal Mast Landing" at Mallison's Falls and driven down the river to the coast, where they were loaded onto special mast ships, which were built with openings in their aft section, specifically to facilitate loading and transport of these logs back to England.

Windham was originally known as New Marblehead, because the first proprietors were from the town of Marblehead on the north shore of Massachusetts. Located on a rocky peninsula, there was even less room for expansion in Marblehead than was the case in other long-established Massachusetts towns, so in 1734, the town petitioned the General Court for a grant of additional land, arguing that the residents were "more numerous than in most towns of the Province, so that they were straitened in their accommodation." This petition was granted, with land bordering North Yarmouth, Gray (then known as New Boston), Sebago Lake, the Presumpscot River and Falmouth, which at the time included what is now the city of Portland. The grant stipulated that sixty-three ten-acre lots were to be laid out in "as defensible a manner as possible." Three lots were reserved for a minister, the support of the church and support for the schools. The sixty settlers on the other lots were required to build houses and establish at least seven acres of grass suitable for supporting livestock. Ongoing conflict with the Native Americans and French prevented much development during the first few decades following the original grant. A sawmill was erected at Mallison Falls, over the objections of the local Indians. The Native Americans, whose name for the falls was *Nagwamqueeg*, claimed ownership of the land on both sides of the river at that point and asserted that the erection of dams would harm their fishery.

This was all taking place during a period of increasing tensions between English settlers and Native Americans, who allied themselves with the French in what is now known as the French and Indian Wars. In 1743, New Marblehead, along with a number of other settlements, was granted one hundred pounds by the General Court to construct a fort. Located on the highest point of land in town (just south of the Parson Smith House on River Road), work was completed in 1744.

The fort is described as being square-shaped, fifty feet to a side. The two-story walls were one foot thick, with small openings just below the second story, which overhung the first by a foot. Two watchtowers, or "flankers," were placed at diagonal corners and equipped with a swivel gun. This entire structure was surrounded by a stockade of posts set in the ground, which was entered through a heavy oak gate secured by bolts and bars. A nine-pound cannon was pointed at this gate.

With the declaration of war between France and England in the spring of 1744, most of the New Marblehead residents moved into the fort. The fort was used extensively during the on-again, off-again hostilities of the following fifteen years. Nevertheless, the population continued to grow, outstripping the capability of the fort to offer protection. Consequently, five houses belonging to Thomas Mayberry, William Mayberry, John Farrow, William Bolton and Caleb Graffam were fortified to resist attack and served as an additional layer of defense against Indian raids.

The need for such protection was very real. Although already decimated by disease and war, there was still a small band of Rockameecooks, a branch of the Sokokis tribe, living on the shores of Sebago Lake. They were led by Chief Polin, who was apparently an effective and determined leader and who became a legendary figure in local folklore. He had petitioned Governor Shirley in Massachusetts for redress of a number of grievances involving the tribe's land and fishing rights but received little satisfaction. On the morning of May 14, 1756, he and a band of warriors laid in ambush, waiting for the white settlers to leave the fort to do some spring planting. They shot and killed Ezra Brown and left Ephraim Winship for dead, scalping both of them. Winship actually survived, with what an early Windham historian described as "a very singular appearance," and eventually fathered eleven children.

The gunfire alerted others, and a small group of white settlers left the fort to engage the Indians. Polin was shot by Stephen Manchester, who had earlier vowed to kill the chief. The Rockameecooks fled the scene, carrying their dead with them. They made their way back to Basin Pond. There, the legend goes, they bent back the roots of a young beech tree and buried their chief underneath, an incident immortalized a century later by John Greenleaf Whittier in the *The Funeral Tree of the Sokokis:*

They heave the stubborn trunk aside,
The firm roots from the earth divide,—
The earth beneath yawns dark and wide.

'Tis done: the roots are backward sent,
The beechen tree stands up unbent,—
The Indian's fitting monument!

When of that sleeper's broken race
Their green and pleasant dwelling-place
Which knew them once, retains no trace;

…O long may sunset's light be shed
As now upon that beech's head,—
A green memorial of the dead!

Locally, this was the last skirmish between the English and the indigenous population, and the defeat of the French at Quebec in 1759 put an end to the threat once and for all.

In 1750, the General Court certified a survey for a new township east of the Presumpscot River, having granted a petition to Captains Moses Pearson and company and Humphrey Hobbs and company, veterans of King George's War. The 39,000-acre parcel included what is now known as Frye Island and Raymond Cape on the eastern shore of Sebago. The township was first known as Hobbs Town, or Hobbs and Pearson Town, for the two main proprietors, but eventually it became known simply as Pearsontown, presumably following Humphrey Hobbs's death. In 1785, it was incorporated as Standish, apparently in honor of Miles Standish of the Plymouth Colony. Because of the tensions with Native Americans, little progress was made during the first two of the three years that were allowed for settlement, and in response to a petition spearheaded by Humphrey Hobbs, the General Court granted an extension to the proprietors. The proprietors also requested that the court provide funds to build a fort, but this request was turned down.

Thirty-three thirty-acre lots were laid out; as with Windham, one lot was reserved for a minister, one for support of the church and one for the

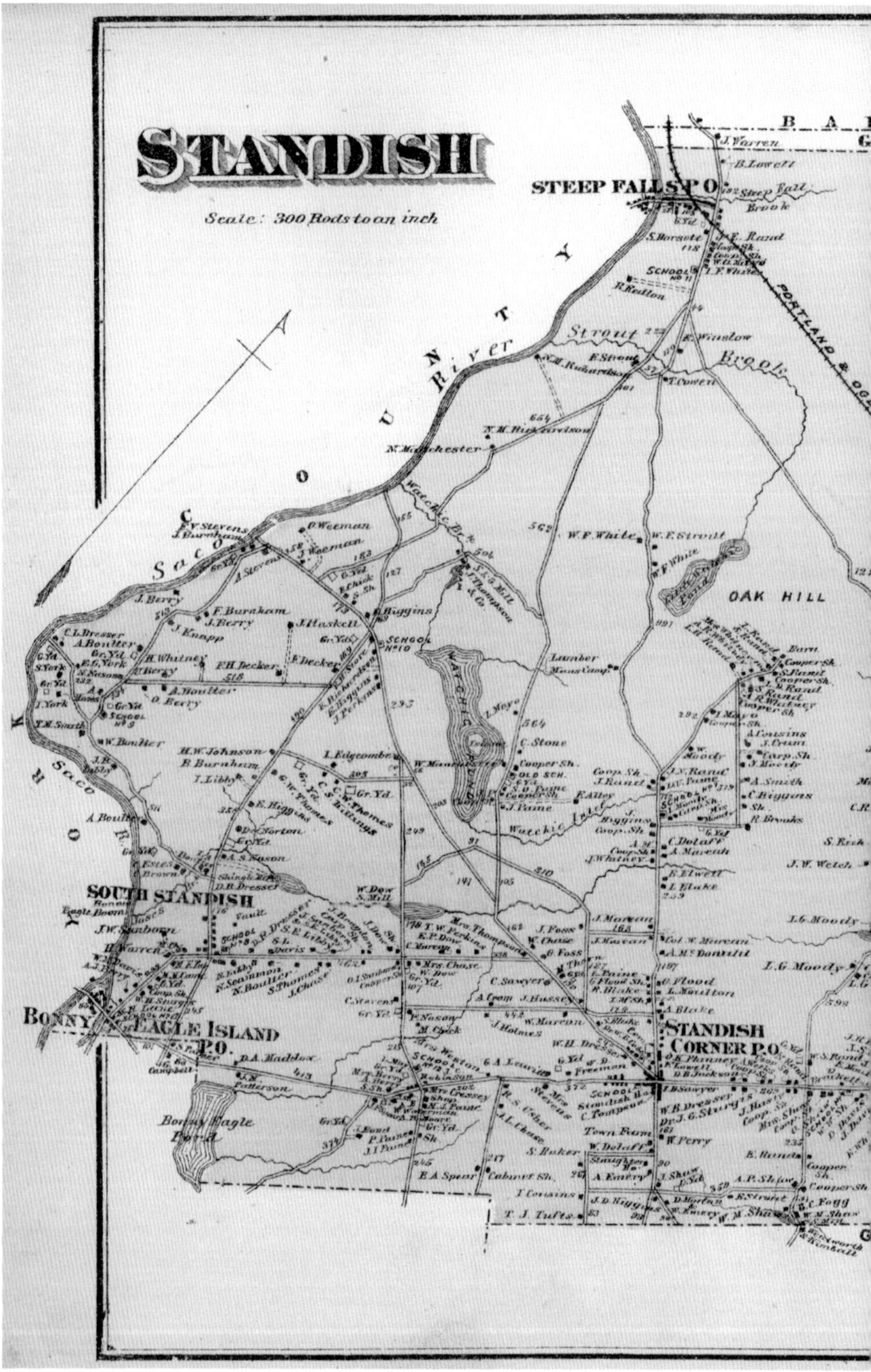

Map of Standish, from *Atlas of Cumberland Co. Maine,* F.W. Beers & Co., New York, 1871.

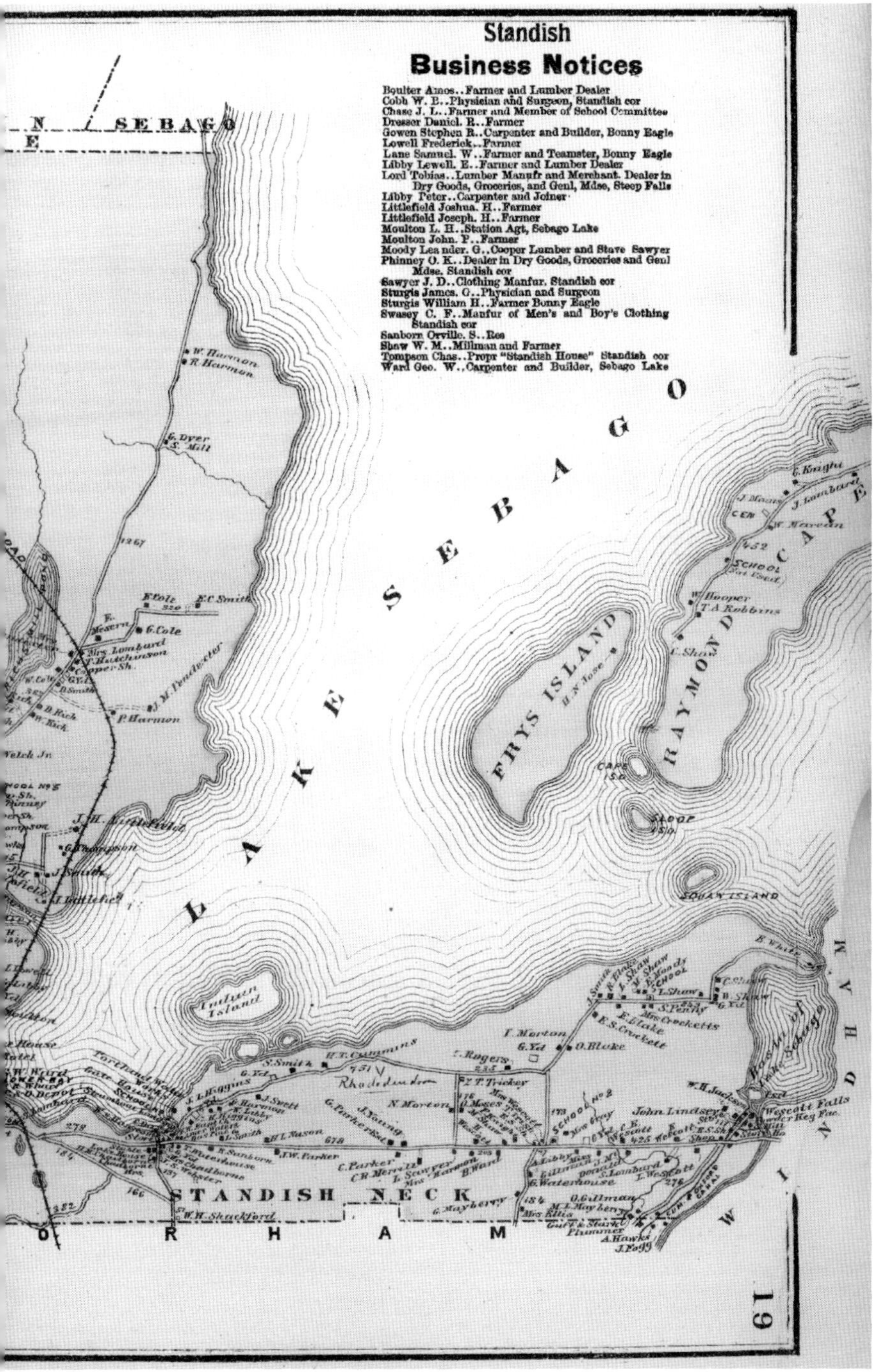
Standish
Business Notices
Boulter Amos..Farmer and Lumber Dealer
Cobb W. B..Physician and Surgeon, Standish cor
Chase J. L..Farmer and Member of School Committee
Dresser Daniel. R..Farmer
Gowen Stephen R..Carpenter and Builder, Bonny Eagle
Lowell Frederick..Farmer
Lane Samuel. W..Farmer and Teamster, Bonny Eagle
Libby Lewell. E..Farmer and Lumber Dealer
Lord Tobias..Lumber Manufr and Merchant. Dealer in Dry Goods, Groceries, and Genl, Mdse, Steep Falls
Libby Peter..Carpenter and Joiner
Littlefield Joshua. H..Farmer
Littlefield Joseph. H..Farmer
Moulton L. H..Station Agt, Sebago Lake
Moulton John. P..Farmer
Moody Leander. G..Cooper Lumber and Stave Sawyer
Phinney O. K..Dealer in Dry Goods, Groceries and Genl Mdse. Standish cor
Sawyer J. D..Clothing Manfur. Standish cor
Sturgis James. G..Physician and Surgeon
Sturgis William H..Farmer Bonny Eagle
Swasey C. F..Manfur of Men's and Boy's Clothing Standish cor
Sanborn Orville. S..Res
Shaw W. M..Millman and Farmer
Tompson Chas..Propr "Standish House" Standish cor
Ward Geo. W..Carpenter and Builder, Sebago Lake
SEBAGO
LAKE SEBAGO
FRYS ISLAND
RAYMOND CAPE
Indian Island
SQUAW ISLAND
STANDISH NECK
GORHAM
WINDHAM
19

school. A committee was formed to lay out a tract of land with a stream suitable for establishing a mill. Difficulties in attracting settlers continued for several years, however. Five-acre lots were established, to be laid out on the plain between Gorham and Sebago Lake. None of these five-acre lots appear to have been settled, and they may never have even been actually laid out on the ground. The next year, the proprietors voted to allow grantees to switch their original thirty-acre lots, but ongoing hostilities with the Indians apparently continued to discourage settlers. In 1754, the proprietors decided to erect a fort at their own expense and appointed a committee of Moses Pearson, Joshua Freeman and James Lunt to oversee the project. Work was nearly completed when it was burned, apparently by Native Americans. Repairs were made, however, and it was opened, probably in 1754. To further protect the residents and encourage settlement, three thirty-acre lots near the fort were re-divided to create eighteen five-acre lots in what is now known as Standish Corner. Conditions remained difficult, however, so Massachusetts agreed to provide two swivel guns and authorized pay and subsistence for fifteen privates, which was a means of supplying assistance to the struggling families through the late 1750s. It appears that all the houses were within the walls of the fort at this time.

By 1762, the situation with the Indians was sufficiently settled that the proprietors were able to entice Ebeneezer Shaw to construct a sawmill on the Little River. This attracted a new wave of settlers, many of whom were from New Hampshire (and not coincidentally, related to Ebeneezer Shaw) and possessed valuable skills. According to Timothy Dwight, whose book, *Travels in New England and New York*, first published in 1821, provides insightful descriptions and commentary on much of the region, prior to 1784 the inhabitants of Standish made little attempt at farming, believing that the climate was

> *so unfavourable, and their soil so sterile, that all efforts of this nature must be fruitless. So by some considerations, or other, they were induced to make a single trial; but with a strong apprehension, that they were labouring in vain. They sowed, and planted, their fields; and were not a little surprised to find them, at the usual period of harvest, covered with good crops. Since that time they have regularly applied themselves to agriculture, and with success. They cultivate wheat, but not in great quantities. Maize succeeds well. Apple-trees are numerous, and thrift; and pear-trees grow without difficulty. The houses were in general ordinary.*

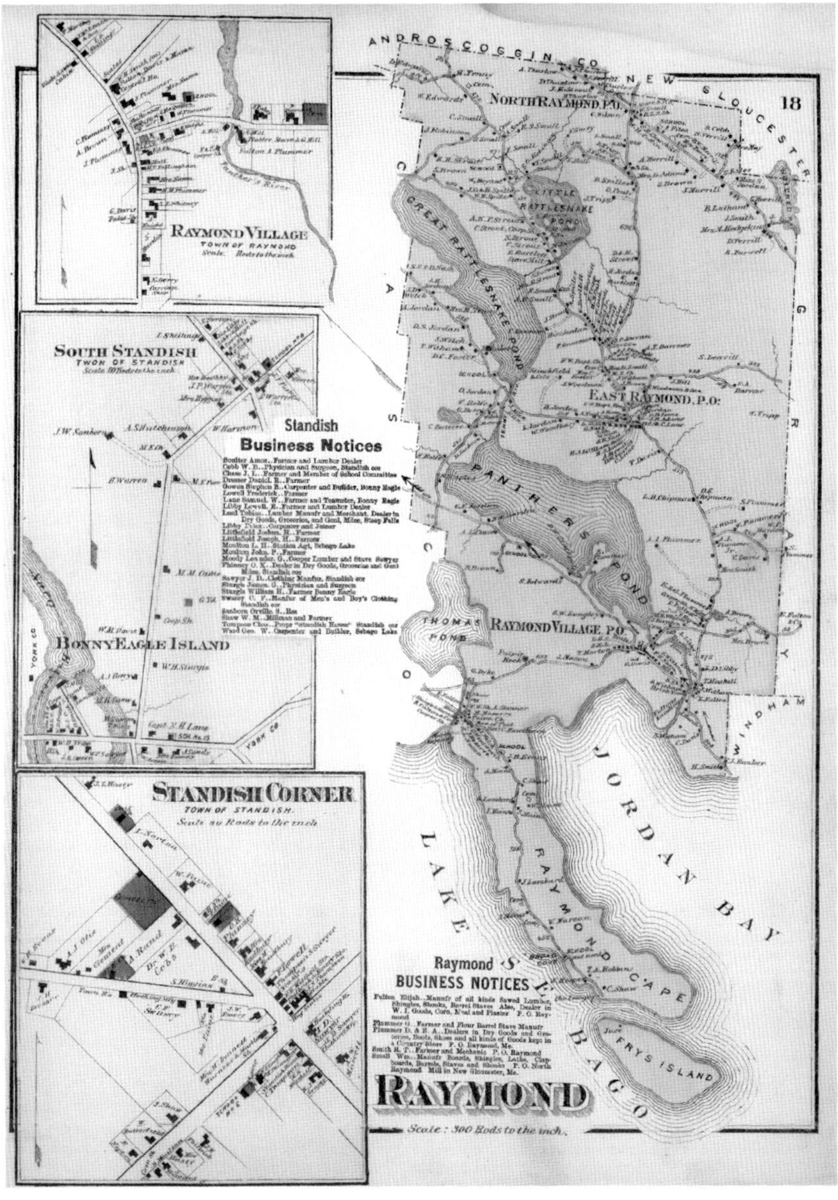

Map of Raymond, from *Atlas of Cumberland Co. Maine*, F.W. Beers & Co., New York, 1871.

Also according to Dwight, it was not until 1787 that loggers began to raft logs across the lakes, having exhausted supplies of timber closer to the Presumpscot River. With sawmills languishing, the lumbermen were without employment and

> *their families saw nothing but ruin before them…Their first attempts at rafting (a thing, which would probably have been thought practicable by no other persons,) were so often unsuccessful, that even themselves were discouraged. But the pressure of poverty, and a spirit of hardy enterprise, induced them, though not without some intermissions, to persevere until they finally completed their design. In consequence of this event, logs in immense numbers were brought to market down the river Presumpscot…The saw mills were repaired, and put into action: and an extensive commerce was opened from Portland in this useful article.*

In 1766, the Massachusetts General Court granted Captain William Raymond and others a large tract of land in compensation for their military services. Known as the plantation of Raymond Town, it included portions of what became Casco and Naples as well.

According to Herbert G. Jones in *Sebago Lake Land*, a brisk rivalry sprang up between Captain Joseph Dingley and Dominicus Jordan, both from Cape Elizabeth, Maine, to be the first to settle in the area and establish a mill. They arrived at Standish Neck and camped for the night, but Dingley, "a shrewd fellow…rose early before dawn, took the canoe, and paddled across the lake to what is now South Casco, and selected his lot." Jordan cut a path along the shore and established a homestead about three miles away, at Jordan Bay, now part of Raymond. Raymond was incorporated as a town in 1803.

As Jean and David Hankins pointed out in *A Short History of Otisfield, Maine*, which they prepared for the Otisfield Historical Society's celebration of the town's 1998 bicentennial, when George Peirce established his homestead and mill on the Crooked River, Otisfield covered a much larger territory than it does today, having lost large tracts to Naples and Harrison when those towns were formed. It was named for Colonel James Otis, one of the original proprietors. Peirce settled in Edes Falls, now part of Naples, apparently building the all-essential sawmill and gristmill. Benjamin Patch arrived in 1776, a year after Peirce, and married George Peirce's daughter Sarah. They moved to Bell Hill, which, unlike Edes Falls, where Peirce settled, is still part of Otisfield.

The town spread out from Edes Falls, which provided ready access to Long Lake, the major transportation artery in the region, as well as the water power to run the mills. Bell Hill, originally known as Otisfield Hill, was settled early, probably because its position on a ridge provided well-drained soil and a longer growing season than the low-lying river valleys. David Ray built the first gristmill and sawmill in what is still Otisfield in 1783 at the

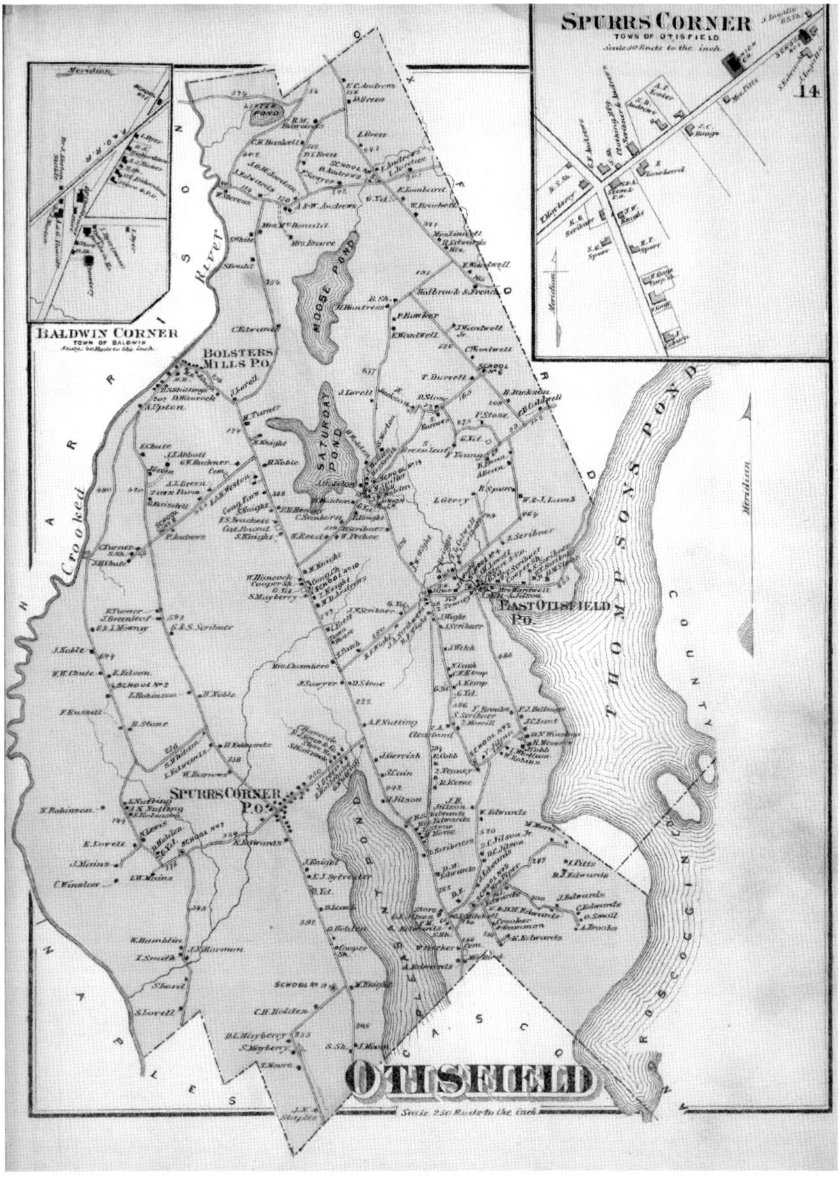

Map of Otisfield, from *Atlas of Cumberland Co. Maine*, F.W. Beers & Co., New York, 1871.

outlet of Saturday Pond in the eastern section of town. Ray was the town's first doctor, opened his own school even before the town's first public school and was elected moderator of the first town meeting. Not surprisingly, the area became known as Rayville.

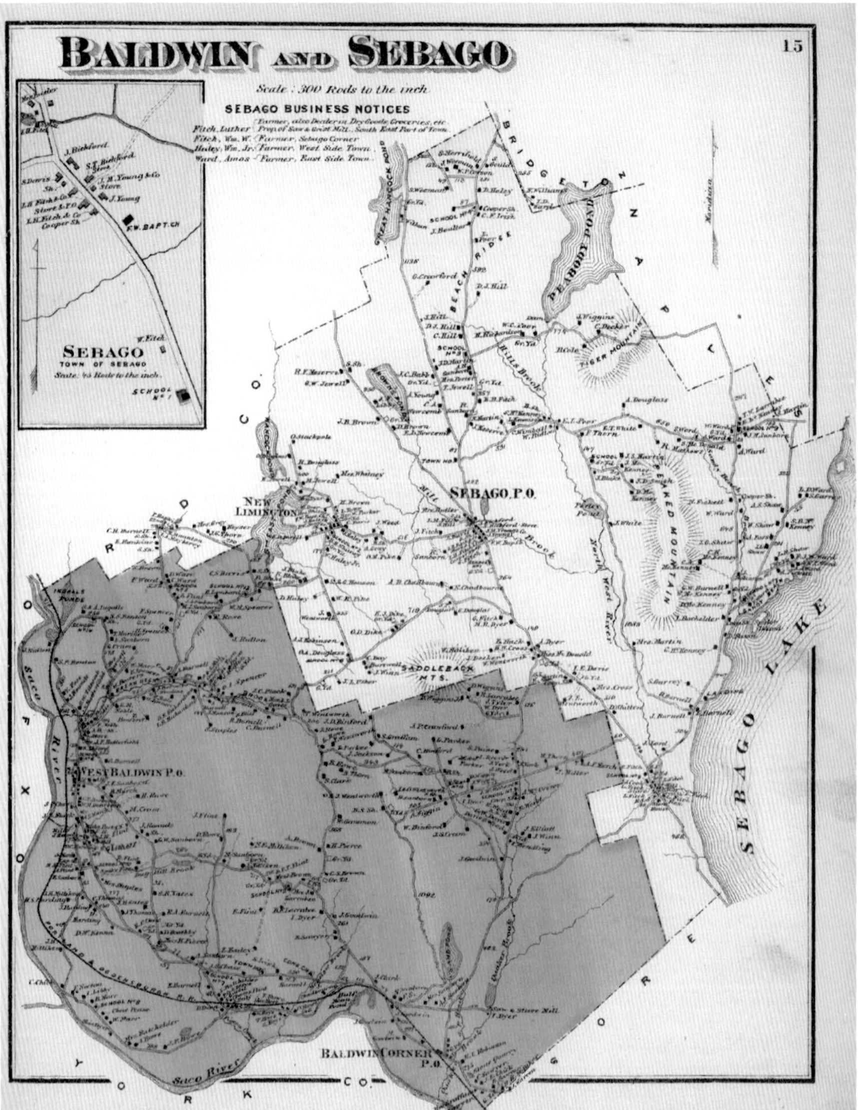

Map of Baldwin and Sebago, from *Atlas of Cumberland Co. Maine,* F.W. Beers & Co., New York, 1871.

In 1787, the settlers successfully petitioned the General Court to gain the status of plantation, which gave them a larger voice in their own affairs, and in 1798, they were incorporated as a full-fledged township. The first meetinghouse was built in Bell Hill in 1797, and the town's first school followed in 1800. Like the region as a whole, Otisfield's population increased rapidly in the next few decades.

In 1780, the Massachusetts General Court granted Captain John Flint and company a tract of land extending from the east side of the Saco River to "Sebago Pond." This grant, known as Flintstown, was made in lieu of an earlier one located between the Merrimack and Connecticut Rivers. It was one of the earlier grants in the area disputed by Massachusetts and New Hampshire. This plantation was incorporated as the town of Baldwin in 1802, and in 1826, the northern part was split off as Sebago.

Joseph Lakin and Jacob Howe are credited with being the first permanent settlers in Sebago. They settled in the neighborhood that later became known as "Hillside," an elevated area like Bell Hill in Otisfield that was considered to be better suited for farming than the poorly drained, boggy low-lying areas. In 1789, Zachariah Fitch, one of the Flintstown proprietors, was awarded a lot, seized for the previous owner's non-payment of taxes, on condition that he build a sawmill there within two years and keep it operating for a minimum of ten years. By 1800, William Fitch was operating a sawmill on this site in the part of town that came to be known as East Sebago. Also by 1800, he was operating a gristmill in Sebago Center. The Fitch family operated a sawmill in East Sebago well into the twentieth century, the gristmill in Sebago Center was still going strong in 1880, and the family operated a general store in East Sebago until the late twentieth century.

The early history of Naples is closely entwined with that of its neighbors, since it was not incorporated as a separate town until 1834. On March fourth of that year, the Maine legislature approved a petition from sixty-six voters who lived in parts of Bridgton, Harrison, Otisfield, Sebago and Raymond who objected to the hardship involved in traveling long distances to their respective town centers for political and business affairs. The town of Naples was formed by taking territory from parts of these five towns. It is said to have derived its name from a similarity between the curve of the bay and that of the Bay of Naples in Italy. At the same time Naples was incorporated, the towns of Denmark and Fryeburg were required to cede a total of 3,700 acres to Bridgton as compensation. This is all territory in what is now considered to be West Bridgton and includes the Shawnee Peak ski area. Casco has a similar history; it was not created until 1841, when a group of citizens from the western portion of Raymond successfully petitioned the state legislature to grant them independent status as a town.

Bridgton, in an area known originally as "Pondicherry," also traces its origins to grants of land in the disputed area of southern New Hampshire

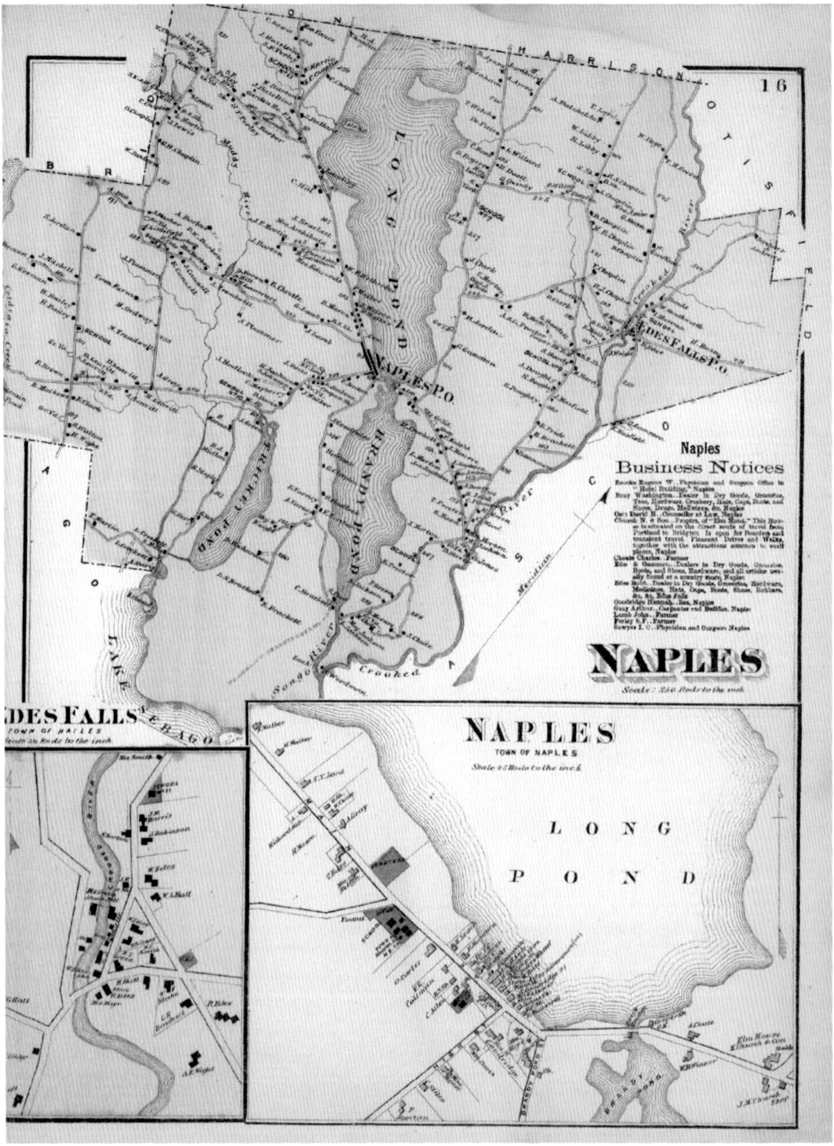

Map of Naples, Maine, from *Atlas of Cumberland Co. Maine,* F.W. Beers & Co., New York, 1871.

and Massachusetts. In 1736, Massachusetts laid out a township and awarded a grant to James Bridges, who had served in a company under the command of Captain John Tyler in 1690, but in 1741, that land was deemed to be part of New Hampshire. James Bridges died in 1739, but his grandson, Moody

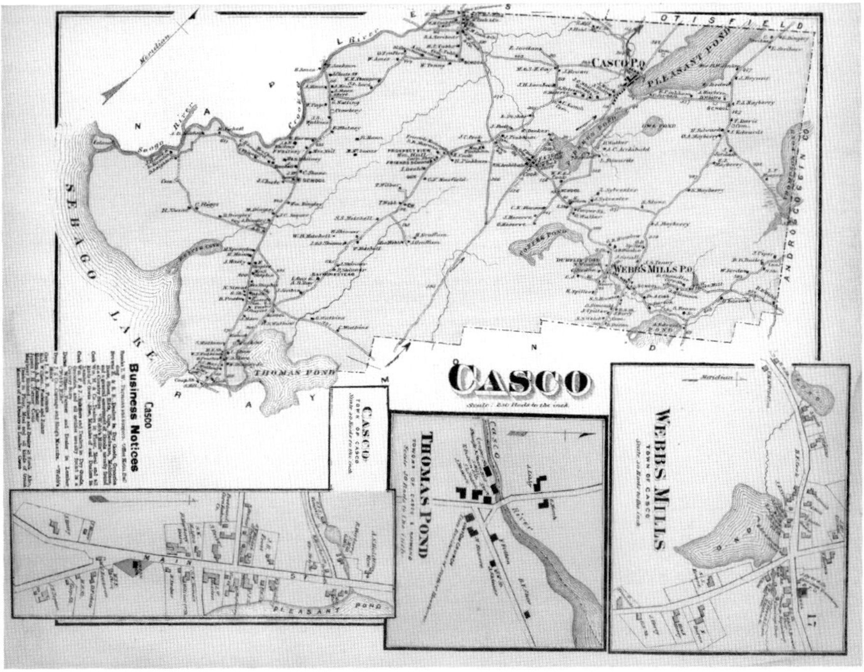

Map of Casco, from *Atlas of Cumberland Co. Maine*, F.W. Beers & Co., New York, 1871.

Bridges, as one of the legal representatives of the original grantees, revived the claim and the General Court awarded the new grant, which would eventually became the basis for modern-day Bridgton.

The first white settler did not arrive until 1768, well after the cessation of conflicts with Native Americans had subsided. He was Benjamin Kimball, who agreed to build a tavern and store on West Cove at Long Lake, in what is now North Bridgton. Kimball, a former sea captain, was also required to operate a boat over the lakes and waterways connecting the southern end of Sebago Lake in Pearsontown (now Standish) with the newly established settlement. With roads all but nonexistent between the Standish/Windham area and Bridgton, this was a much-needed service that must have greatly facilitated settlement of the region.

The Bridgton proprietors also found a man to build and operate the all-important sawmill and gristmill. Jacob Stevens built his house and mills at the foot of Crotched Pond (later renamed Highland Lake), by the outlet of the brook that now bears his name as it winds through the center of town. Stevens had been a member of the survey crew headed by Solomon Wood that laid out the township, and he had intimate knowledge of the land. He

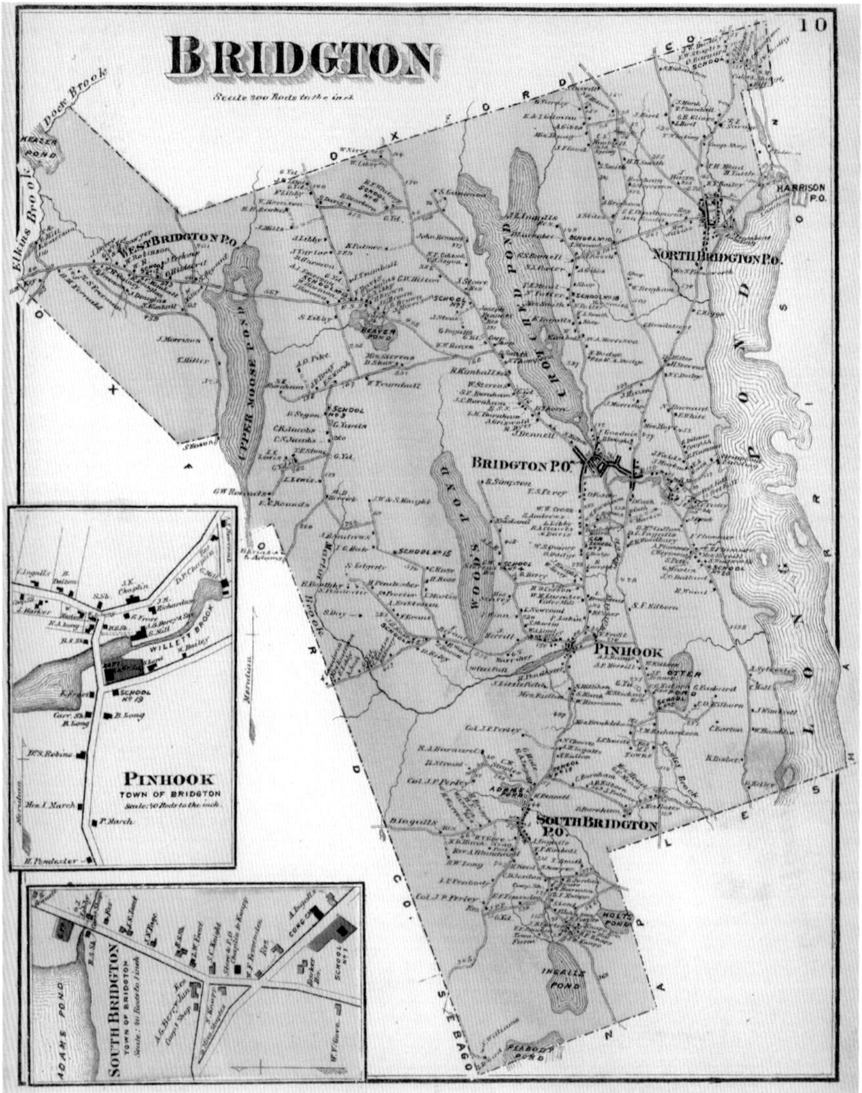

Map of Bridgton, from *Atlas of Cumberland Co. Maine*, F.W. Beers & Co., New York, 1871.

bought many lots and established some rough roadways. In summer, these roads were strewn with obstacles such as stumps, rocks and mud holes. Snow cover leveled them off in winter, when they were easier to negotiate, but transporting both the logs he needed and the finished boards he produced remained a challenging task. Even so, settlers as far away as Waterford (on the other side of Harrison from Bridgton) used boards from his mill in their

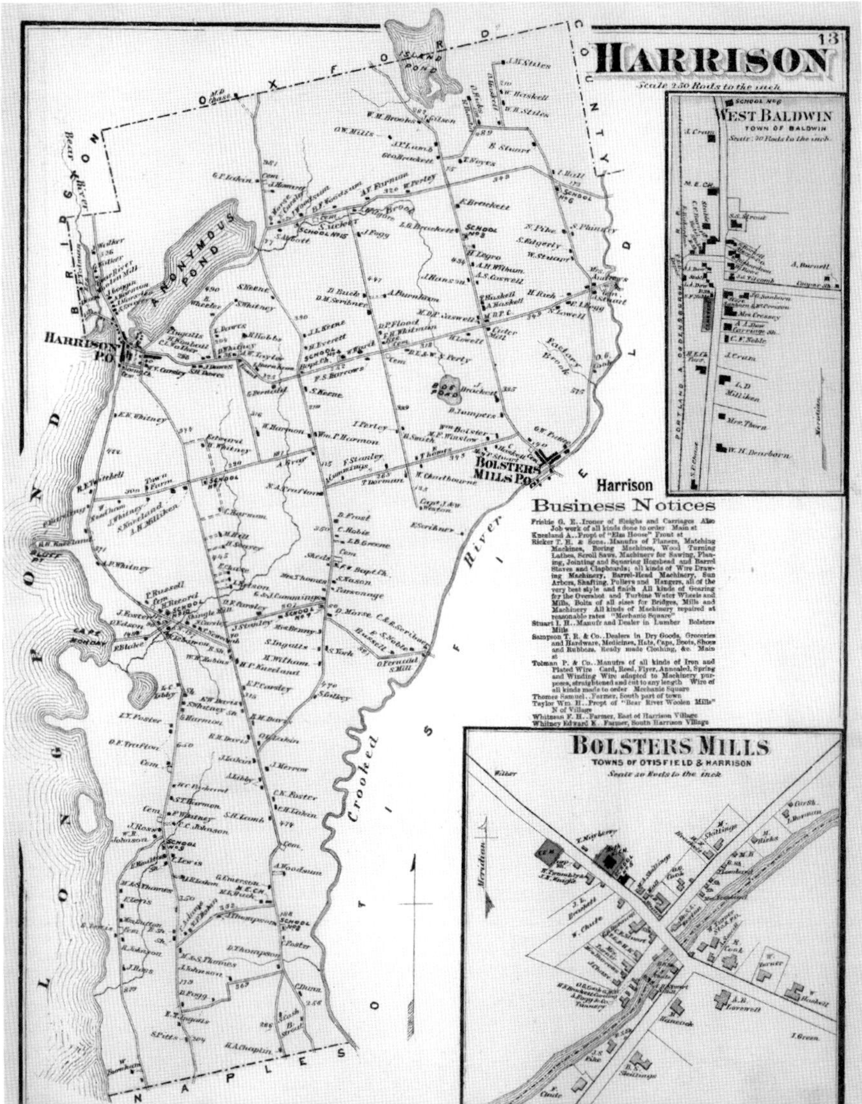

Map of Harrison, from *Atlas of Cumberland Co. Maine*, F.W. Beers & Co., New York, 1871.

houses as late as 1790 and took their grain to his mill to be ground. For every hundred pounds of grain, the settlers took back fifty pounds of ground meal, with the remainder going to the miller as payment. Bridgton was already establishing itself as something of a commercial center. In the century that followed Stevens's death in 1802 (the same year Jacob Kimball died), Stevens

Brook, with at least ten power sites on its short journey from Highland Lake to Long Lake, would produce the energy to run lumber mills, textile mills, gristmills and other manufacturing facilities, making the town a bustling center of industrial activity.

The two-volume *Bicentennial History of Harrison, Maine, 1905–2005*, compiled by the Harrison Historical Society, is a great source of information about the history of the town. Harrison was formed from the portion of Bridgton that was east of Long Lake and the portion of Otisfield that lay west of the Crooked River. Both of these areas were remote from their respective town centers, and in 1805, the Massachusetts General Court granted petitioners from these locales the right to form their own town. Inexplicably, a portion of the village of Harrison that lay north of the outlet of the Mill Stream into Long Lake remained with Bridgton until 1867, when the Maine legislature rectified the situation and transferred the land to Harrison.

John Carsley Jr. and his brother Nathan were the first white settlers on the land that became Harrison. They arrived from Gorham in 1792, building a camp on Maple Ridge and beginning the process of clearing the land. John Carsley did not remain in Harrison for very long (although he is buried in town, and his gravestone identifies him as Harrison's first settler), but Nathan and his wife, Susie Cotton Carsley (the first white woman in the area), were lifelong residents, with direct descendants in town in the twenty-first century. The first settler in the central village area was James Sampson. Originally from Duxbury, Massachusetts, he moved from Leeds around 1800 and built a dam at the outlet of Anonymous Pond, establishing the all-important saw and gristmill.

This first wave of white settlers in the Sebago Lakes Region inhabited a sparsely populated district, but even in the early nineteenth century, the area was not an isolated backwater. Prominent families enjoyed a lifestyle not unlike that of their counterparts in Portland, which was then a major shipping center with ties that reached literally around the world. Evidence of this can be seen in the collections of Bridgton Historical Society's Peabody-Fitch House, known as "Narramissic" (the name given to it by its last private owner).

The house was built by William Peabody in 1797 in South Bridgton. William Peabody, born in Andover, Massachusetts, in 1770, was the son of Deacon John Peabody and Mary (Perley) Peabody. The Perleys were arguably the most prominent and influential family in Bridgton at the time, so both sides of William's family were well-to-do. A number of original family pieces, purchased from the Pocumtuck Valley Memorial Association of Deerfield, Massachusetts, in 1991 and returned to the house, are identical or similar to items that belonged to the

Federal candle stand, made by the Radford Brothers in Portland, nearly identical to one in the Wadsworth-Longfellow House. *Collections of Bridgton Historical Society.*

Longfellows, McLellans and other prominent Portland families. The Perleys, who lived in a house just down the road, had their portraits painted by the well-known artist John Brewster (reproductions hang in the house today), and the Perley girls attended a fashionable school for young ladies in Portland. A letter from Mary Perley to her mother, Sarah, in 1825 describes meeting the Marquis de Lafayette at a reception she attended when the famous French hero visited Portland.

In 1790, the population of the Lakes Region stood at just 1,654; by 1820, it had risen to 10,468, more than a six-fold increase. It continued to rise steadily until around 1850, when it stood at 17,637. By then, most of the political boundaries and settlement patterns had been established. The pioneers had successfully carved their settlements and communities out of the frontier, establishing a system of town government, churches, schools, trade, commerce and many other amenities of western society. But if this growth and prosperity were to continue, that crucial link to Portland and the outside world had to be maintained, and much of the story of the middle decades of the nineteenth century revolves around attempts to maintain that link.

Chapter 2

OPENING TO THE WORLD

The Canal and Railroads

THE CUMBERLAND AND OXFORD CANAL

Since travel by land during the eighteenth and early nineteenth centuries was difficult and ill-suited for transporting freight, waterways were the primary means of transportation. There were a number of waterfalls along the Presumpscot River, which made for difficult navigation between the Sebago Lakes Region and the busy commercial center and harbor in Portland. It is not surprising that there was interest in building a canal along this route. In 1795, the Massachusetts General Court incorporated a group that included several Portland merchants to serve as proprietors of the Cumberland Canal, and in 1804, Loammi Baldwin, a prominent Bostonian and one of the proprietors of Flintstown (which later became the town of Baldwin) surveyed a fifty-mile canal route to Portland. Unfortunately, the economic downturn precipitated by Thomas Jefferson's Embargo of 1807 dealt a severe blow to these plans.

By 1820, demand for such a connection had grown again, and in 1821, Maine's first governor, William King, granted a charter to Albion K. Parris and others to build the canal. A committee consisting of Woodbury Storer, John Perley, Phineus Varnum and Eli Longley issued an enthusiastic report, estimating the cost of construction at just under $131,000 plus 5 percent for unforeseen contingencies. The corporation issued stock, and the legislature authorized a lottery to raise $50,000 for the project. Raising the necessary capital still proved difficult, and in 1825, the legislature chartered the Canal

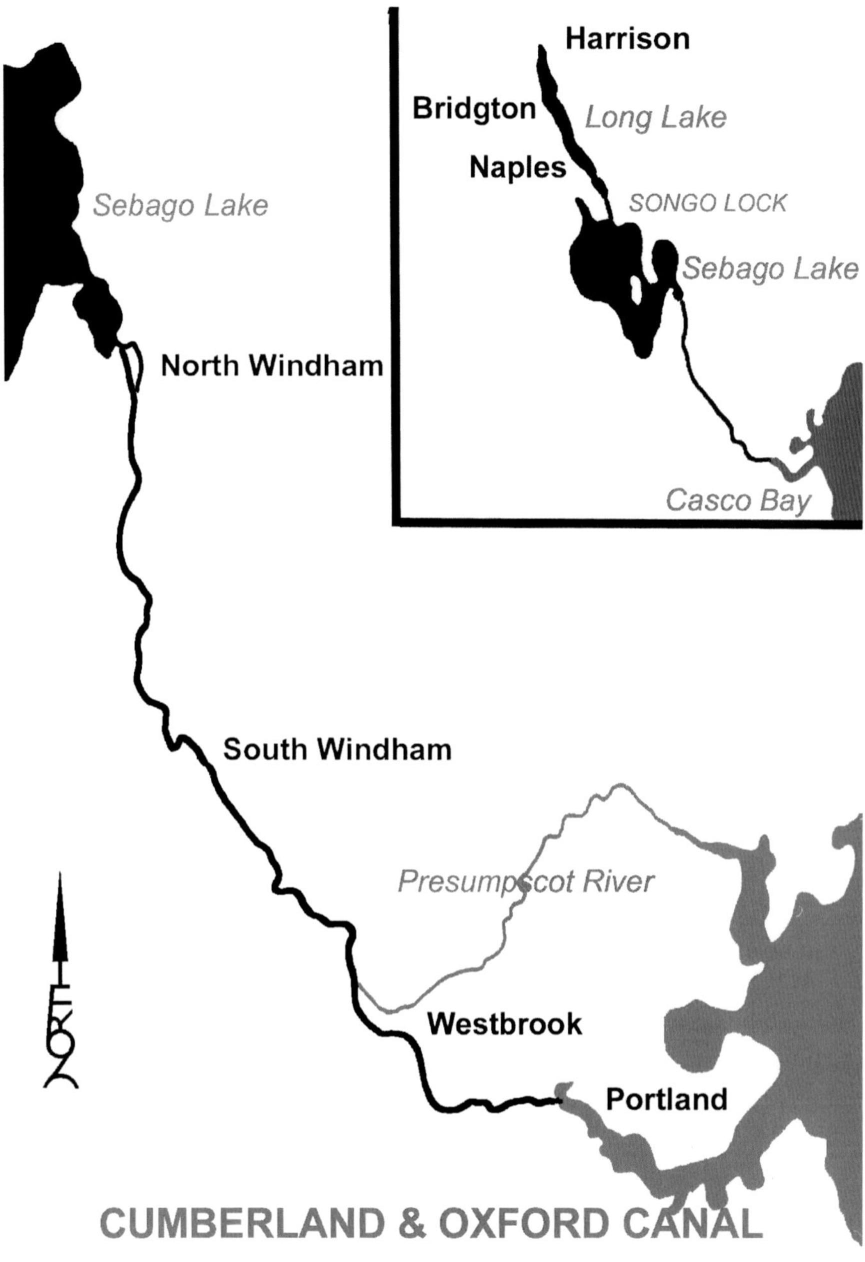

The heavy black line shows the route of the Cumberland & Oxford Canal, which connected the Lakes Region to Portland harbor. *Adapted from a map on Wikipedia.*

Bank, authorizing it to invest 25 percent of its $300,000 capital in the canal. The bank also made numerous loans to the canal and, in the end, provided over 70 percent of the funding. At $220,000, the actual construction cost was well above the original estimate, which meant that the canal began operating with a debt that was in the neighborhood of $90,000. Deficit spending is not an exclusively twenty-first-century phenomenon.

Construction began in 1828 with Irish laborers, digging with shovels and picks and moving the excavated earth by hand or oxen. Ledge was blown with gunpowder in a slow and dangerous operation. The canal finally opened in June 1830, when a number of VIPs traveled the length of the canal on the *George Washington*, which was built as an excursion boat by William A. Rive of Great Falls. A few days later, the first loads of cordwood reached Portland. The boats were generally sixty to seventy feet long and five feet deep, drawing twelve to eighteen inches of water, with a capacity of as much as thirty tons. To ensure that vessels could pass through the locks smoothly, these dimensions were tightened slightly and standardized by the corporation in 1834. No boats over sixty-four feet long or nine feet, eight inches wide could be registered.

The boats were towed through the canal itself by horses on sixty or more yards of line, and they were poled through Basin Pond, the Songo River and the channel in Naples. Crewmembers pushed the poles into the bank or bottom and walked from bow to stern along a narrow gunwale just one foot wide. In the open lakes, the boats relied on their sails and were surprisingly fast and stable. The original square-rigged design was replaced with fore and aft sails and two centerboards. Hayden Anderson, in *Canals and Inland Waterways in Maine* (from which most of this material is derived), described an incident involving the canal boat *Columbia*.

> *Delayed in Portland by a break in the canal, several boat crews joined in trimming that venerable craft for speed, with ample canvas and barely enough ballast for good handling. The Columbia then sailed to Peaks Island in a spanking breeze, showing her square heels to everything in the harbor, to the amazement of island watchers. "She surprised them critters terrible," Dan* [Scribner] *said.*

The canal quickly became an important transportation link for Lake Region merchants. One problem, however, was that it did not operate during the winter, and freight over land was more expensive even during the winter, when sleighs could be used on the roads. In late fall, the merchants tried to

This photo, which dates to circa 1870, is believed to be Plummer's Landing, on Long Lake in Bridgton. The vessel at the far right is a canal boat. *Courtesy Bridgton Historical Society.*

put in a winter's supply of goods before the canal froze. Bridgton storeowner Dixey Stone reportedly ordered five barrels of rum in November each year but ordered one per month from April through October.

Passenger service was not an important part of the canal's business, although a few passengers were carried from time to time. The *George Washington*, which was built as an excursion vessel, was not economically successful and was used strictly for hauling freight. No doubt the lack of passengers can be explained at least in part by the fact that the trip through the canal was an extremely slow one, and it was said that anyone in a hurry could do better by walking.

There is a firsthand account of a trip on the canal in the collections of the Museum of Fine Arts, Boston, titled "Up the Canal to the Mountains." It was written by the artist John Bradley Hudson (1832–1903) about an expedition that he took with fellow artist and friend Charles Frederick Kimball (1831–1903). It paints such a vivid picture of the experience that it is worth recounting and quoting at length. The two left Portland, bound ultimately for Mount Washington, on August 6, 1859:

> *It was six o'clock at night when the driver started his horse to tow us up; winding around Bramhall's hill, the canal being built close to the shore. Passing under Vaughan's bridge and across the basin we came to Stroudwater village where were some tide mills…On approaching a lock the driver gives two or three peculiar shouts, raising his voice and holding*

the last note for a long time. This was to arouse the keeper, who lives near, and is obliged to open the gates when a boat approaches; when within the lock the lower ones [gates] *are closed, and the large plank slides open in the upper, through which the water rushes in perfect sheets, splattering over the bows and surrounding us with foam.*

Soon the boat begins to rise and in a few minutes is on the level with the water above. All hands now jump on shore and help open the gates, leaning their backs against the projecting part of it and their feet against pieces of wood placed around in circles, stepping backwards from one to the other until they [the gates] *are opened wide enough for the boat to pass through.*

About seven we were invited to the cabin to supper. A room some six feet square and about the same height, it contained a cook stove, hanging table, two broken chairs, chests, buckets and a collection of cooking utensils. On two sides were sleeping berths.

Our supper consisted of hot biscuit, applesauce and tea. During the evening we sailed quietly along…At ten o'clock we stopped for the remainder of the night.

As there were not enough berths, he was invited to sleep with the captain but found that "the place was anything but inviting, the [bed] clothes looking as if they had never come in contact with soap and water." He was woken "by the buzzing of mosquitoes and a sense of being bitten by bugs." Soaked in perspiration, he went on to write, "Sleep vanished from my eyelids and I passed the remaining hours until daylight in perfect misery."

In the morning, he went on shore and walked ahead of the boat. That this was not a rapid means of transportation is underlined by the fact that he walked so far ahead that he was able to sit and sketch until the boat caught up with him. At the head of the canal, they hoisted sails to cross the pond. "The sails were full of holes and there was a strong breeze which whisked through them at a fearfull [*sic*] rate. I expected every moment to see them torn from the masts, but they held on while we went through the water at great speeds." Their boat was not going beyond White's Bridge at the foot of Sebago Lake, so they waited for another. When they saw one coming, they hired some boys who rowed them out to it. This boat was nearly new "and in every way superior to the one we came up in," and they were able to sail along "at a rapid rate." They passed an uneventful and apparently more comfortable night.

Sunday morning all hands were called to help work the boat up river. This had to be done by poling as it is called. They have long poles with one end

> *padded and the other pointed iron. First placing the pole perpendicularly, they send it with a quick motion to the bottom, then lean with their shoulders against the padded end and walk toward the stern as the boat moves along, leaning forward so as to touch the rail where their hands were. We found upon trial that even this work required some practice, as we were unable to throw the pole to the bottom. When placed for us and we had walked to the end of the boat with it, could not get it out of the mud again.*

This was the Songo River, notorious for being crooked. The crew pointed out a tree that they passed five times before losing sight of it. He wrote, "So short were some places that the boat touched the shore on both sides in turning." After passing through the final lock (Songo Lock), they entered Brandy Pond, where they were able to hoist sail and move along at a rapid clip again. They got off in Naples and set off on foot for Bridgton. In fact, most of this trip is on foot, a remarkable fact to the twenty-first-century reader. They walked all the way to the foot of Pleasant Mountain, several miles west of Bridgton, before stopping for the night. Although they generally slept in their tent, they obtained most of their meals simply by stopping at farmhouses and asking. At one house, he commented, "The supper was excellent but the lady of the house was not very gracious until we offered to pay for it. She then became as pleasant as possible during our stay." People frequently mistook the two for peddlers, often calling out to inquire what they were selling. This also apparently explained the reluctance of some to come to the door when the travelers came by looking for a drink of water or a meal. Although the nineteenth century witnessed revolutionary advances in transportation, it is clear from this description that travel by the most basic means possible, on foot, was practiced to an extent that is almost incomprehensible today. Even so, toward the end of journey, after leaving the town of Sebago headed toward Portland, they found the way "tiresome and uninteresting," and Hudson commented that "the day being excessively hot and the road hard and dusty," their feet were so badly blistered they found it difficult to walk. They stopped at noon in Gorham and "rested until the train arrived about four o'clock, which we took and were soon with our friends, having been absent just two weeks, and walked two hundred miles."

The canal appears to have been busiest from its opening through 1852, when it collected $16,500 in tolls, its best year. The late 1830s showed some decline as a result of wider economic difficulties, but the real decline set in during the 1850s. In 1850, the Atlantic and St. Lawrence Railroad came to South Paris. This line served points in Oxford County on its way from Portland to Montreal and probably took some of the canal's business. At about the same time, the York and Cumberland Railroad was built, eventually passing through to New Hampshire and connecting to points west. In the 1850s, it went as far as Saco, which siphoned off much of the canal's business from Westbrook and Gorham.

The canal started out with $90,000 worth of debt and spent most of its life teetering on the brink of failure, and competition from the railroad was probably the straw that broke the camel's back. One contemporary, Solomon Cloudman, whom Anderson cites in *Canals and Inland Waterways of Maine*, even felt that the canal was simply a failure, arguing that very few individuals benefited, while vast sums were wasted and productive land was destroyed. Cloudman, as Anderson points out, did not have a particularly objective perspective on the question, since his family had lost productive farmland when the canal was built, receiving essentially worthless stock in return. But even given its considerable financial problems, it is hard to argue that the canal did not make an important contribution to the development of the Sebago Lakes Region. The canal served as the outlet for large quantities of freight during its heyday, providing access to markets for the region's products and contributing to the region's prosperity, as well as enhancing the fortunes of already prominent and successful families such as the Fitches, Perleys and Plummers.

From the late 1850s on, the Cumberland and Oxford Canal faced increasingly difficult challenges, and its final years seem to have been basically an attempt by its owners to salvage some financial gain from it in any way possible. In 1862, it was sold to Isaac Dyer of Baldwin and F.O.J. Smith of Portland. By the end of the Civil War, it was in a state of disrepair, and in 1867, Luther Fitch leased it. This arrangement ended in a lawsuit, with Dyer suing for money that Fitch held back as payment for supervising the canal and accounting for the tolls, the net profits of which were to go to the canal. The court allowed Fitch $640 and Dyer just over $100. Other unsuccessful strategies for extracting some money from the canal included ice-cutting operations and the creation of a huge fish-breeding facility. Following the deaths of Dyer and Smith in the 1870s, General Charles Mattocks, Dyer's stepson, became the owner of the canal. The failure of William Bradstreet's proposal to run the narrow-gauge railroad along the canal route (described below) and a similar proposal for a streetcar line effectively ended any hope for its survival.

THE NARROW-GAUGE RAILROAD

By the 1870s, Bridgton was a local commercial center, with a considerable amount of industrial activity, and was starting to become a tourist destination. But without a railroad, it was in danger of being left behind. The Atlantic and Saint Lawrence Railroad (originally the Grand Trunk), which had been built to connect Portland with Montreal, making Portland Montreal's winter port, went through Norway, about fifteen miles northeast of Bridgton. To the west, the Portland and Ogdensburg, which later became the Maine Central Railroad, went through Hiram and Fryeburg, about fifteen miles south and west. In Bridgton, teamsters, the owners of livery stables, blacksmiths, wheelwrights and others involved with horse-drawn transportation may have fared reasonably well during the 1870s, which saw a national economic downturn. However, as it became clear that trains were to be the preferred mode of transport for both passengers and freight, mill owners and other businessmen who depended on the efficient movement of goods and raw materials were increasingly isolated from their markets and suppliers. Under the circumstances, it is not surprising that there was growing interest and agitation for bringing a rail line to Bridgton.

Construction of a railroad was an expensive proposition for a small town, but the success of the narrow-gauge Sandy River Railroad in central Maine showed that it could be done. The term "narrow gauge" refers to the distance between the rails. Standard gauge rails are four feet, 8½ inches apart. There have been numerous narrow-gauge lines used throughout the world, of varying sizes, but in Maine they were just two feet apart, some of the smallest in regular service. There were a number of advantages to using a narrower gauge. It was less expensive, since less iron was required, and since it was smaller, it was lighter and easier to install. The narrower gauge also made tighter curves possible, which made it easier to negotiate the steep terrain that characterizes much of the region.

Various routes were proposed. Some suggested that the line should run up the east shore of Sebago Lake through Westbrook, Naples and Raymond. Others favored a route to Portland that utilized the towpath of the Cumberland and Oxford Canal. Still others pushed for a route running northeast, to South Paris, via Harrison and Waterford, where it could connect to the Atlantic and St. Lawrence. The route that was finally chosen went to Hiram, where it connected to the Portland and Ogdensburg Railroad.

As was often the case, the decision as to which route to choose was surrounded by conflict and controversy. In 1879, A.G. Bradstreet, a civil engineer and a representative to the Maine legislature, proposed an "Act granting permission…to locate and construct a railroad from Bridgton to some point on the Portland and Ogdensburg or Portland and Rochester Railroads." Initially this line was to be called the "Bridgton & Presumpscot River Railroad," with an estimated cost of less than $250,000.

Little was done for two years, but in 1881, a public meeting was held at the Town House in Bridgton, which was addressed by Major Henry A. Shorey, publisher of the *Bridgton News*, and other prominent citizens. A ten-member committee was appointed to investigate ideas for a railroad and prepare a proposition for a town meeting. A mass meeting on February 28, 1881, was sharply divided over the route. Bradstreet was given the approval to proceed with constructing the direct route to Portland, but the proposal contained what we might now call a "poison pill:" he had to raise $250,000 in just ninety days. Unable to raise what was then a prodigious sum in such a short time, he gave up his idea of the direct route and moved to Colorado, where he became involved with three-foot narrow-gauge railroad lines.

On July 30, 1881, the Bridgton and Saco River Railroad was formally created. The backers of the project reached an agreement with the Portland

Interior of a passenger car on the Bridgton and Saco River Railroad. *Courtesy Bridgton Historical Society.*

and Ogdensburg over division of joint receipts: 75 percent was to go to the Bridgton and Saco River, until its share was $10,000 more than the Portland and Ogdensburg's. After that time, the two lines would share equally in the receipts. The Bridgton and Saco River was responsible for reloading expenses. Reloading was necessary because the cars of the two lines traveled on different-sized rails, so they could not be transferred from one line to the other. The freight had to be transferred by hand at "Bridgton Junction," as the Hiram station was called. A special siding was constructed, with narrow-gauge track and standard running side by side.

Not surprisingly, conflicts over the route continued even after the decision was made to run through Hiram. F.H. Brown and others in North Bridgton continued to fight for a route that would go through Harrison and Waterford, via North Bridgton. They succeeded in throwing up legal roadblocks to issuing the bonds, but finally a large town meeting in March 1882 voted to proceed with the Hiram route. Local disagreements sprang up even after the big decision regarding the terminus was made. J.R. "Uncle Joe" Foster, who operated a sawmill, shook shop (which produced the wooden staves for making barrels) and store in South Bridgton, protested that the proposed route did not go to the center of South Bridgton. Although the steepness of the grade made such a route virtually impossible, he swore that he would never use the railroad, proclaiming, "I'll haul freight from Japan with a rooster first."

S.L. Stephenson of Gorham was the chief engineer charged with surveying the route, which ran from Hiram through the towns of Sebago and Denmark before entering Bridgton. Stephenson accomplished the task in eight weeks and two days. The first shovelful of earth was turned at Hiram on July 17, 1882, by Stephenson and Joseph A. Bennett, chairman of the Bridgton Board of Selectmen and one of the prime movers behind the railroad. By mid-October, the Bridgton depot was nearly finished. Millard M. Caswell was appointed master mechanic, and he remained with the railroad for forty-two years.

Construction of the line greatly changed the landscape in some areas. For example, the Sandy Creek or "Pinhook" neighborhood in Bridgton was changed so drastically that a notice in the *Bridgton News* speculated that if the "good departed citizens of Pinhook come back to earth they would hardly recognize the Sandy Creek of today." Still, the railroad's arrival was cause for great celebration, and Charles O. Stickney, reporter for the *News* and one of the early historians of Bridgton, waxed poetic with the following lines after the first of the little trains chugged into town late in the afternoon on Saturday, January 21, 1883:

Engine number 8 pulling what appears to be a "railfan" excursion near the end of the little railroad's life. *Courtesy Bridgton Historical Society.*

And hark! through the valley o'er hillside and plain
The thunder is heard of the Narrow-Gauge train
And cheers and huzzzas from the spirited throng
Greet the advent of Progress now booming along
"Eureka!" the shriek of the engine declares,
And "Bridgton Redeemed" is the motto it bears!

The railroad made two major contributions to the area, as a freight carrier and as a passenger service. The many mills in Bridgton and other communities along the line were now in a much better position to do business, both for shipping their product to market and for obtaining the materials and supplies they needed to produce their goods. Inbound trains carried coal, used by houses and mills, and grain for horses and other livestock, as well as food, merchandise and other goods that were not produced locally. Outbound trains carried wood and lumber products, woolen products, apples and other agricultural produce. Unfortunately, the freight rates were relatively high, especially for farmers and smaller manufacturers.

The line also played a major role in opening up the area to summer people and other visitors "from away." Two forty-five-foot wooden coach cars, the "Pondicherry" and the "Mount Pleasant," designed by the Laconia Car Co. in New Hampshire, were elegantly appointed with polished brass, ornate

Ticket used on the narrow-gauge railroad in 1898. *Collections of Bridgton Historical Society.*

lamps, coat hooks, carved oak walls, window frames and fancy iron seats with mohair upholstery. Initially, the railroad operated separate runs for freight and passenger service, but once business settled in at a steady level, the trains were run with both passenger and freight cars. There were three round trips daily during the summer and two during the off-season, and in 1893, the little trains carried a total of sixteen thousand passengers. In addition to the two passenger cars, there were two engines from the Hinckley Works in Boston, a caboose, ten flat cars, five boxcars, a "wedge" snowplow and a "digger" car for plowing snow between the rails. In 1892, a third locomotive, built at the Portland Company just forty miles away, was added.

In the 1890s, the Westbrook, Windham and Naples Railway started making plans to extend its electric streetcar line along the eastern shore of Sebago and Long Lake all the way to Harrison. In response, the Bridgton and Saco River sought permission to extend its existing line the additional five and a half miles to Harrison. This permission was granted in 1897, and on August 3, 1898, the first train ran to Harrison, with a stop at North Bridgton.

In the ensuing years, the line continued to prosper, adding more locomotives, up to a total of eight. In 1912, the Maine Central Railroad, which by that time had succeeded the Portland and Ogdensburg, bought the balance of the Bridgton line's shares (it had owned one hundred shares since the founding of the B&SRR). The line did well for the next decade or so, reaching its high-water mark in 1921, taking in a total of $112,000, $80,000 of which was from hauling freight, to net $23,000.

However, by 1925, the little railroad's fortunes had radically changed. Improved automobiles, trucks and buses, and the roads they traveled on, cut significantly into its business. Astonishingly, as owner of the Samoset

A narrow-gauge train at the Harrison station. The line, which originally terminated in Bridgton, was extended to Harrison in 1898. *Courtesy Bridgton Historical Society.*

Bus Company, the Maine Central Railroad actually competed with itself, by operating buses from Portland up the Roosevelt Trail (Route 302) to Bridgton and Harrison. With lower revenues, the narrow-gauge railroad line was unable to maintain its equipment properly. Two engines failed to pass inspection and were retired, and the operation was cut back to one train per day, which left Bridgton in the early morning. The following year, the company defaulted on payment of the bond interest. At a mass meeting in July, townspeople claimed that the Maine Central had deliberately sabotaged the company. They voted to re-take ownership, and the town of Bridgton acquired the line for $27,000, forming the Bridgton and Harrison Railway, which officially took over operations in 1930.

Thanks to the Maine Central Railroad's failure to upgrade the tracks to Harrison to handle heavier locomotives, a rain-softened sag in the bed derailed engine #8. With less freight business and even fewer passengers from Harrison, that branch was abandoned, just a few short years after the railroad was renamed the Bridgton and Harrison.

To save money, the pared-down line began operating with an unattractive, homemade, gasoline-powered "railbus," which was fashioned from a 1927 Chevrolet body. This was replaced by another railbus, which was acquired from the Sandy River Railroad when it went out of business in 1936. This

The Bridgton & Harrison Railroad Railbus at the Bridgton Depot. This unusual vehicle kept the railroad going throughout much of the 1930s. *Courtesy Bridgton Historical Society.*

three-axle vehicle was a vast improvement over the Chevy. The switch to the railbus, which hauled a small boxcar trailer, proved to be an efficient way to run the line and helped to extend its life through the entire decade of the 1930s. During this period, boys' and girls' camps provided an important boost to business each summer, and rail enthusiasts were already coming to Bridgton to see and ride on the famous two-foot railroad.

Even so, the future of the struggling line was not a bright one. In 1939, Bertram Scott, chairman of the Bridgton Board of Selectmen, led an attempt to abandon the railroad. A sparsely attended town meeting that year voted to sell for any price in excess of $20,000. A larger meeting was held later, but it upheld the earlier decision. Portland attorney James McNutt was appointed to carry out the sale. He immediately revealed that a salvage dealer from Newburyport, Benjamin O. Checkaway, had deposited $20,001 to make the purchase. There were a series of attempts to thwart this sale, which did not appear to have been carried out in good faith, but they were all unsuccessful. The last train ran on September 7, 1941.

With the prospect of war looming on the horizon, the rail went to the U.S. Navy. Shortly after the sale to Checkaway, it was revealed that almost all of the rolling stock and equipment had been purchased by Ellis D. Atwood of South Carver, Massachusetts. Atwood was already operating a two-foot tramway to serve his large cranberry-growing operation. With the Bridgton equipment, he expanded this into a tourist attraction and railroad museum, which he called the "Edaville Railroad." In 1993, the Edaville sold much

One of the last of the passenger cars is ignominiously hauled out of Bridgton after the railroad was shut down. *Courtesy Bridgton Historical Society.*

of its equipment, including the Bridgton and Saco River Engines #7 and #8 and other rolling stock, to the Maine Narrow Gauge Railroad Company and Museum in Portland. This organization's mission is to preserve Maine's industrial and railroading heritage, and the little trains that once connected much of the Lakes Region to the outside world run as educational and cultural attractions around the Portland waterfront on a regular basis. As of this writing, the Maine Narrow Gauge Railroad Company and Museum is exploring the possibility of moving most of its operation to another location. Although Bridgton was seriously considered, Gray now seems the more likely candidate to host the enterprise.

Chapter 3

MAKING A LIVING

Agriculture, Business and Industry

Agriculture and the Rural Economy

As we have seen, the lakes, rivers and streams were the major transportation routes for early settlers and remained so through the first half of the nineteenth century. Once the mills and stores had been established, most of the immigrants to the area carved their farms out of land on elevated ridges, where the first frost in the fall is likely to be a bit later and the last in spring a bit earlier. In addition to having a slightly colder microclimate, many of the low-lying areas were boggy and poorly drained. The differences may have been slight, but they were apparently enough, at least in the minds of the settlers, to justify the choice.

The land was cleared by the slash-and-burn method. Ideally, trees would be cut in the early summer and left, with the leaves on, to dry. The leaves helped to spread the fire. Any logs left would be piled or put in rows and burned, with the ashes enriching the soil. If all went as planned, the land could be planted in the spring. Stumps were pulled by oxen, although there are also accounts of farmers planting around the stumps. If the timing of the burn was off or there was not a good burn, the farmer might have uncleared, partially burned logs to deal with as well. The next step was removing the rocks, which of course were plentiful, and building the stone walls that have become such an iconic part of the landscape of the Lakes Region and New England as a whole. The presence of so many stone walls running through what is now dense woods is testimony to the far more open landscape of the nineteenth century. After all, no farmer was building a wall through the woods. Any area enclosed by stone walls was once an open field.

Livestock roamed freely at first, but this practice was apparently being curtailed by the 1790s. In 1794, for example, Bridgton voted to construct a pound to hold stray domestic animals until they were claimed by their owners. It was replaced by a more robust pound ten years later, when the town voted to construct a pound that was "26 feet square and 8 feet high with 13 posts 8 inches by 10 inches, sills 12 inches square, set on stones one foot below ground and 8 inches above ground; a good gate with lock and key." In Raymond, the pound was similarly substantial: Ernest H. Knight, writing in *Raymond Then and Now*, published by the Raymond Woman's Club in 1978, describes it as being made of six-foot high split stone, thirty feet square, with an oak gate. He comments that this "should have been adequate to restrain the most rambunctious stray."

From settlement in the late 1700s through the early 1800s, farming was very much a subsistence activity. In the early days, almost everyone, even those living in a village and operating a business or other professional concern, did some farming. Outside the villages, farms were usually between one hundred and two hundred acres, with a variety of crops, including corn, hay, wheat and other grains, root crops and an assortment of vegetables. Most farms had a few sheep, supplying wool and meat, cattle, a horse, pigs and oxen, which provided most of the power for plowing, hauling timber out of the woods and other such tasks. Horses did not begin to be used for such purposes until the late nineteenth century, when more sophisticated and lightweight equipment was manufactured. The use of oxen appears to have persisted longer in the Lakes Region, and horse-drawn equipment was still not unusual as late as the 1930s.

Farms were often clustered in small neighborhoods, frequently with family ties among at least some of the homesteads. While each farm was an independent entity, raising a diversity of crops and livestock, typically each family might supply a special skill or service, such as blacksmithing or carpentry, or perhaps they owned a particular piece of machinery that would be shared among the different farmsteads. Throughout much of the nineteenth century, buildings in the Lakes Region were constructed using a method that came over with the English and had been little changed for centuries. The frame was constructed of large, hand-hewn beams, as opposed to the balloon framing and two-by-four or two-by-six stud construction that became nearly universal later on. Timbers were cut, squared and carefully fitted together with mortise and tenon joints, secured with wooden pegs,

As late as the 1930s, some farmers were still using horse-drawn equipment, as in this photo from the Pike-Allen Farm in Sebago. *Collection of the author.*

known as trunnels (literally "tree nails"). Each section, or "bent," was put together on the ground and raised into place. Cutting and fitting the timbers was a special skill practiced by a housewright, but the raising of the frame required large numbers of people, and a barn or house raising was often a major neighborhood event.

In *Big House, Little House, Back House, Barn* (University Press of New England, 1984), Thomas Hubka produced an architecturally-based social and cultural study of connected farm buildings, the uniquely northern New England phenomenon of sprawling farm complexes connecting the house and barn through a series of ells and attached sheds. The Sebago Lakes Region lies at the very heart of the geographical area that contains the highest concentration of these buildings. Designed around the daily and seasonal patterns of work, these buildings were intended to make the farm more efficient and profitable. Typically, the barn and outbuildings created a south-facing dooryard that provided a sheltered space for farm activities. Hubka views the structure of these complexes as a result of an essentially functional approach to architecture and actually part of the movement for agricultural reform and improvement. For a variety of reasons, this reform could take place only within the context of

A crew of timber framers, apparently with a building frame ready to be raised, in the Bridgton area. *From a stereo view in the collection of Bridgton Historical Society.*

the traditional mixed-farming, home-industry system. At a time when Midwest farmers were able to efficiently concentrate on raising one primary crop, New England farmers, thanks to hilly terrain and thin, depleted soils, continued to rely on a diversity of crops, augmented by lumbering and the home manufacture of shoes, clothing, barrels and other products. Professor Hubka argues that these connected farms reflect the mutuality and communality that characterized this system, upon which rural nineteenth-century northern New England depended.

Farmers' individual diaries and account books testify to this system of barter and shared work, which was the basis of the economy throughout much of

The Darwin Ingalls farm in South Bridgton, an example of the connected farm buildings of the region. *Courtesy Bridgton Historical Society.*

the nineteenth century. For much of the period, there was simply not a lot of currency in circulation, and the value of what currency there was was based on the value of the metal itself, not the face value of the coin. This barter system, however, rarely consisted of a straight one-for-one swap, which is the way we often think of such arrangements. It would probably more accurately be described as a credit (or debit) economy. A customer did not just walk through the door of a general store with four chickens and a couple pounds of wool to trade for a new hat. Instead, goods were accepted by the shopkeeper and credited to the customer's account according to their monetary value, and the goods the customer took away were charged against his account, again according to their monetary value. This was actually a rather efficient system, since it did not depend on two people having exactly the product or service that the other one wanted. If you needed a new broom, for instance, you didn't have to find a broom-maker who happened to be in need of cheese or whatever else you had to offer. It wasn't even necessarily required that you bring something with you to the store. You just went to the store, where the shopkeeper had

Loose hay piled high in the barn at the Pike-Allen Farm, in Sebago. *Collection of the author.*

taken brooms in trade and had also taken your cheese. And the shopkeeper might take your cheese to Portland, where he would trade it for manufactured or more exotic goods not available locally.

These accounts, which often involved labor as well as goods, were running accounts that were not settled on a regular basis. Most ran for years before being balanced. Settling accounts was often the result of a move out of town, a sudden need for cash or to settle an estate following the individual's death. These transactions were recorded in account books, which were used by both individuals and businesses, to keep track of all this. Often daybooks were used to record transactions as they took place and are arranged chronologically. These transactions were then transferred to an account book, which was arranged according to the name of the other party—a customer, in the case of a storekeeper's account book. Today, they provide valuable insights into the economy and daily life of previous centuries.

Although every farm seems to have had at least one "milch cow," milk was not generally drunk as a beverage, as it is today. The farm wife strained the milk into earthenware pans that were set in the cellar, a springhouse or other cool place. She skimmed off the cream when it rose to the top and made it into butter. The skimmed milk was fed to livestock or made into cheese. Excess dairy products could be used for barter at the general store to acquire some of the few imported or manufactured products.

By the late 1800s, more and more people were living in cities and towns and not keeping a cow or raising food as they had been a generation earlier. This meant that the market for agricultural goods was expanding, in spite of a decrease in farmers and continued deterioration of the soil's fertility. In 1889, the Bridgton Creamery Company was formed. Herbert Berry went to visit the creamery in Turner, Maine, where he learned how to operate the four horse-power steam engine and six horse-power boiler that was used to produce butter. Farmers now strained their milk into tall cans that were put into tanks of ice water, with the milk being drawn from the bottom and the cream transferred to another can, which was collected twice per week. This also increased the demand for ice, which was harvested in the winter from ponds and lakes and stored in sawdust in icehouses.

Apples, many of which were pressed for cider, were a mainstay for New England farm families, and the topography and climate of the Sebago Lakes Region was well adapted for their production. Writing in *Ninety Years of Living*, his memoirs of growing up in the 1840s and '50s on what is now the Bridgton Historical Society's "Narramissic," the Peabody-Fitch Farm, Edwin Peabody Fitch, who moved west after the Civil War, wrote, "I shall never forget the apples, such apples as California will never have."

The orchard at Five Fields Farm, just up the road from the Fitch's farm, had its start in 1928 when John T. Gyger Sr. first planted apple trees in South Bridgton. By 2011, the property was still in the Gyger family, and it included a commercial orchard with a pick-your-own operation, along with cross-country skiing in the winter. For several years, the farm has hosted

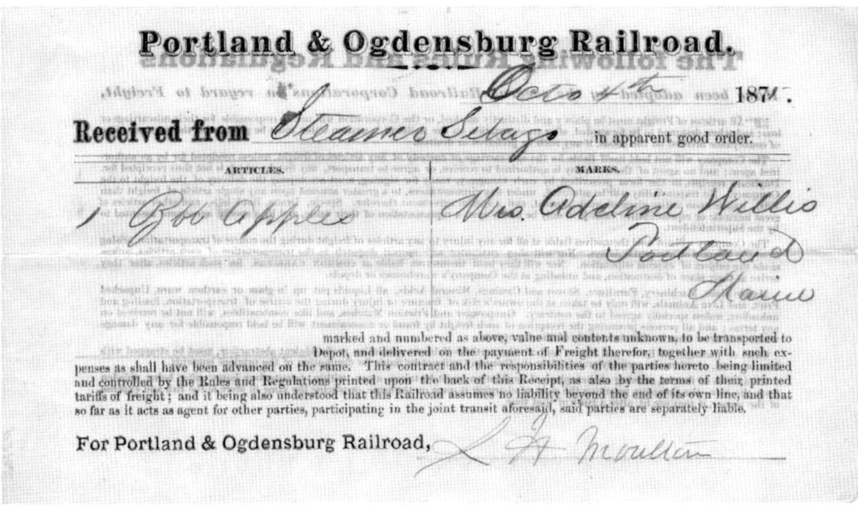

Portland & Ogdensburg Railroad.

Octo 4th 1874.

Received from Steamer Sebago in apparent good order.

ARTICLES.	MARKS.
1 Bbl Apples	Mrs. Adeline Willis Portland Maine

marked and numbered as above, value and contents unknown, to be transported to Depot, and delivered on the payment of Freight therefor, together with such expenses as shall have been advanced on the same. This contract and the responsibilities of the parties hereto being limited and controlled by the Rules and Regulations printed upon the back of this Receipt, as also by the terms of their printed tariffs of freight; and it being also understood that this Railroad assumes no liability beyond the end of its own line, and that so far as it acts as agent for other parties, participating in the joint transit aforesaid, said parties are separately liable.

For Portland & Ogdensburg Railroad,

Receipt for shipment of apples on the Portland and Ogdensburg Railroad and the steamer *Sebago*, 1874. *Courtesy Bridgton Historical Society.*

the "Musher's Bowl" sled dog races, which became a major weekend on Bridgton's winter event calendar. In nearby Sweden, Maine, Pietree Orchard is establishing an organic orchard operation. With a dramatic hilltop setting, it carries on a tradition started by the McSherry family on that spot in the 1930s, and in South Windham, Apple Acres Farm continues a farming tradition started by the Johnson family in 1949. This farm now includes a gift shop and commercial cider press. Like the Gyger's at Five Fields Farm, the Johnsons have diversified to include some non-agricultural activities, putting on an annual bluegrass festival and hosting other family-friendly events.

INDUSTRY

Even a predominantly agricultural area supported a certain amount of industry, and the Lakes Region has been home to a surprising number of mills and manufacturing firms throughout the years. Most of them were dependent on locally produced raw materials—generally wood, animal and plant products. They also relied on local energy, which for much of the nineteenth century meant water power, which was in ample supply.

This began, of course, with some of the earliest white settlers. As we have seen, one of the first requirements for newly settled areas was the establishment of a gristmill and sawmill. In Windham, settled earlier than most of the region, Joseph Knight was operating a sawmill by 1756. Knight's mill was located at Mallison Falls. His sons, Joseph and Nathaniel, operated the sawmill until 1823, when a Portland group purchased the property. They formed the Casco Manufacturing Company in 1824 and built a cotton mill. This appears to have spurred the town's development, bringing new residents to work in the mill. The company built housing for some of the workers and operated until fire destroyed the building in 1856. The site was not redeveloped until 1875, when C.A. Brown & Co. purchased it and built a sawmill. A gristmill and carding mill were also part of Windham's early history.

At another site in Windham, on the Pleasant River, which feeds into the Presumpscot River, Major Edward Anderson built a large sawmill. Dissatisfied with the amount of power available, he created an outlet from Collins Pond, which empties into the Pleasant River via Smith's Brook. Eventually, the artificially increased volume of water undermined the dam, and on June 14, 1814, it created a huge flood, undermining two mills that Anderson had constructed on Smith's Brook, along with a sawmill, a gristmill, four bridges on the Pleasant River and two on the Presumpscot.

In 1861, another Windham dam gave way. This one had just been completed in 1860, apparently with insufficient underpinnings. Frederick Howard Dole was employed as a clerk by Oliver and Joseph Pope, the owners of the dam, and described the incident in vivid detail in his book *Sketches of the History of Windham, Maine, 1734–1935*. The Popes ignored repeated warnings by knowledgeable townspeople, and refused to believe that there was any threat to their enterprise. In Dole's words:

> *The news of the outbreak spread rapidly through the town, and several hours before the flood came hundreds of men came with offers of assistance in removing goods and machinery, but the owners steadily refused to allow this to be done…*
>
> *At about ten o'clock, a low, sullen roar, like the rushing of a mighty wind, gave evidence that the hour of peril was near at hand; and in a short time, around a curve in the river came an immense wave bearing on its crest a large quantity of debris, consisting of stumps, the ruin of bridges, mill logs, cord wood and trees that had been torn up by the roots, all in one confused mass, and borne along with irresistible force by the rushing waters.*

Parts of the newly constructed mill complex were swept away, and the rest was flooded as high as the second floor, ruining the machinery and much of the manufactured cloth stored there. About a fourth of a mile downstream, a "well-appointed sawmill belonging to Josiah S. Allen" was "said to be the best and most firmly constructed of any similar building in town. Having withstood the flood for some time, it was at length lifted bodily from its foundation, and floated out of sight apparently unharmed, and with the chimney standing. At some distance below, it was dashed into a thousand fragments by the mad rush of the torrent." Dole went on to report that most of the bridges downstream on the Ditch Brook were carried away, and bridges on the Presumpscot sustained heavy damage.

Gambo Falls, upstream from Mallison Falls, was another early Windham mill site, with a gristmill and sawmill operating under the management of Jonathan Leavitt, starting around 1769. The river separates Windham from Gorham, and a carding mill for processing wool was opened on the Gorham side in 1816. The next year, Lester Laflin and Edmund Fowler, both from Southwick, Massachusetts, purchased the water rights on the Gorham side and built a line of powder mills. They started to manufacture gunpowder in

1818. They continued to do so until 1827 when, along with their foreman, Matthew McCully, they were drowned in an accident on Sebago Lake. In 1833, Oliver Whipple from Lowell, Massachusetts, bought the property, along with the water rights on the Windham side, and built a new set of mills. Whipple was a shrewd businessman, but he died suddenly and was succeeded by his brother James. Although James appears to have lacked Oliver's savvy, the firm continued to operate until an explosion in 1855 destroyed the mill, killing James and six others. The property was sold to G.G. Newhall & Co., which repaired the damages and erected mills on the Windham side. In 1859, the company was incorporated as the Oriental Powder Co. Not surprisingly, the mills ran around the clock during the Civil War. The Newhall family continued to own the factory, which operated until the depression of the 1890s. The property passed through several ownerships, but by the 1930s, the powder mills had all been torn down, leaving just a small mill manufacturing wood flour, which is used in the manufacture of dynamite. The powder mills were not without their costs, as one can imagine. Explosions were fairly common: Dole states that between 1828 and 1901, forty-five men were killed, and many more severely injured. He quotes a description in the diary of Jonathan Leavitt, who lived in the neighborhood: "The Powder mill at Gambo blew off and seven blowed off: Their names are as follows: Josiah Clark, Hanson Irish, Major Mains, Wm. Moses, James Green, Noah Babb, and Daniel Moses Badly burnt… all dead."

According to Dole, Little Falls, the next above Mallisons, was "one of the best on the river and was improved for manufacturing purposes at an early period in the history of the town." Farther upstream, at Great Falls, Zebulon Trickey was the first to operate a mill, where a sawmill was running before 1800. Shortly thereafter, Enoch White had a large sawmill there, which he operated with multiple saws, which was a new innovation in the field and was very successful. His brother John White purchased the business and continued to operate it successfully. In 1842, furniture maker Walter Corey of Portland built a factory for the manufacture of chairs near the bridge. Corey's business was very successful (his name is well-known to local historians, curators and furniture collectors to this day), and he enlarged the mill, doubling its capacity and employing many workers. At its peak, it turned out twenty thousand chairs each year. Corey sold the business in 1870, and two years later, the mill burned. It was not rebuilt, and in 1896, a large dam was erected to produce electricity. By 1914, the Cumberland County Power and Light Co. owned the rights to the waterpower on both the Gorham and

Windham sides of the river here. Since far fewer employees are required for the production of electricity than for manufacturing purposes, this facility had less impact on the local economy.

"Old Otisfield" (by which is meant the original territory of Otisfield) is an interesting case study in the story of the small and medium-sized mills that operated in the Lakes Region during the nineteenth century. There is evidence that the first mill that George Peirce built at Edes Falls (now in Naples) did not operate on a continual basis during this early period. William Samuel Spurr's *A History of Otisfield* speculates that there was a period of time around 1780 when it was not in operation, since the Spurr family, who lived nearby, were carrying their grist to Captain Dingley's mill in South Casco, ten miles away. The Edes Falls mill may have been destroyed by a spring freshet around 1795 and rebuilt, but by 1797 it had been abandoned. The mills were rebuilt for lumbering in 1827 by Colonel Thomas Edes. In the 1870s, Robert Edes purchased the property, rebuilding the dam and expanding the mills, employing as many as one hundred men. He died in 1889, and although the mills operated sporadically for a time, they were eventually abandoned. There were a number of small mills scattered throughout this area. David Ray built another sawmill and gristmill at the outlet of Saturday Pond. It was operating by 1781 and continued in operation under several owners until 1890. Elsewhere, George W. Barrows operated a tannery until 1839, when he sold the property to Joseph W. Holden, who rebuilt the dam and established a sawmill that operated until 1864 or thereabouts. Several other small tanneries had operated in town since the very early days of settlement. Other mills in Otisfield could be found in Jugtown, at the lower end of the Long Meadows, and at Smith Book; at Spurrs Corner, where Samuel Spurr built a shingle mill around 1850, at the outlet of Moose Pond, where Barnabus and David Sawyer operated (appropriately enough) a sawmill around 1812; and at Muddy River, where, in 1826, Stephen Barker built a sawmill. There were also mills in Otisfield at Pugsleyville, Pinhook and Pleasant Pond, although the latter was built in the 1890s and did not survive very long.

In Sebago, the Northwest River Canal Corporation was formed in 1811, to connect Peabody Pond with Sebago Lake. A series of chutes and dams were constructed, although the enterprise does not appear to have been successful, and accounts for the name of the district, which is known to this day as "the Folly." Around 1830, Daniel McKenney Jr. and his brother Silas built a sawmill on the Northwest River in this neighborhood. They were apparently the first in Sebago to process hemlock, previously considered to be commercially worthless. However, their mill was by no means the first in town. As discussed earlier, by 1800, William Fitch was operating a sawmill in East Sebago and a gristmill in Sebago Center. The Fitch family name was a strong presence in town for the next two centuries.

If there is an area of economic activity that has remained constant since the earliest days of European settlement, surely it must be lumbering. There were more than a half-dozen sawmills in Casco alone during much of the nineteenth century. Water-powered mills became obsolete, but the industry did not disappear. By the early twentieth century, Willard Libby, Willard Chute and M.S. Hancock were all operating busy sawmills. Mr. Hancock alone had five mills in operation in 1940, providing an income for approximately three hundred workers. By the end of the first decade of the twenty-first century, Hancock Lumber was still prospering. It had become a six-generation, family-owned business, one of the nation's oldest family-owned lumber companies. Hancock Lumber not only saws lumber, but it also owns and harvests woodlands and operates a small chain of retail lumberyards and building-supply stores.

In Bridgton, the Bisbee Sawmill, which was originally the Bridgton Lumber Company, was operated by Harry Bisbee until July 1953, when the facility burned with such ferocity that the box factory across the brook was threatened. The only mill building still surviving in Bridgton is the old Smith Mill, or "Coffin Shop," as it is sometimes referred to, for one of its products. It was founded by Lewis Smith, who moved to Bridgton in 1868, and also manufactured furniture, doors, sash and other building components.

Fortunately, Scribner's Mill, located in Harrison on the banks of the Crooked River, has been preserved and provides us with a unique opportunity to see what one of the early water-powered mills was like. Elijah Scribner and his son Cyrus bought the mill shortly after its construction in 1847. Cyrus operated the mill until the mid-1880s, when his sons Bourdon and Jesse took over. Jesse remained at the mill until he was ninety-three, in 1963. The mill originally operated with an up-and-down saw, which is an early design for water-powered mills, and was converted to a circular saw in 1884. A wooden log haul-in wheel was used for the mill's entire 114-year operational life, but other modernizations were undertaken. The original water wheel was replaced with a more modern one in 1896, and in 1916, a small wheel was installed to generate electricity for the mill and the house.

Scribner's Mill Preservation, Inc., was formed to preserve and restore the water-powered sawmill. When the restoration is complete, the organization plans to open to the public to demonstrate the antique machinery and the goods it created by actually using the early technology for the manufacture of wood products. When restored, the mill will operate from early April through November, producing products for the restoration specialty market. These materials will be unique in that they will be produced on authentic machinery and be suitable for museum-quality restorations. The facility will be used as an educational center with programs for students, tourists and residents.

The presence of the Cumberland and Oxford Canal, combined with the large number of potential sites for water power on the area's numerous rivers and streams, opened up many possibilities for the development of manufacturing in the region. In Harrison, a wire factory was established on Mill Brook in 1854 and was an important source of employment until the early 1890s. Water power at Bolsters Mills on the Crooked River, which straddles Harrison and Otisfield, ran a number of mills from 1819 until 1936, when a sawmill on the Otisfield side of the river was destroyed in a flood. A tannery, gristmill, fulling mill and carding mill all operated on the Harrison side in the nineteenth century.

We don't often associate small rural towns with industry, but the Lakes Region seems to have been full of such manufacturing concerns. There was even a brief flirtation with iron mining in Casco during the 1880s, but it proved to be too costly to separate the iron ore from the granite it was mixed with to be financially feasible. In 1849, Luke Brown, who moved to Bridgton from Boston, bought the Beamon Mill in North Bridgton. He set up a furniture business that his sons Freeman and George took over. It operated as Luke and F.H. Brown after 1878. It was best known for making spool and cottage furniture, and it prospered for a number of years. Nearby, also in North Bridgton, the Kitson Pottery operated from about 1815 to 1887. Richard Kitson founded the business after he purchased land along the shore of Long Lake, with the right to dig clay, in 1809. Kitson and his son Richard T. Kitson, who took over the business in 1859, produced redware, a utilitarian household type of pottery. They made bowls, covered pots, milk pans and other useful items, usually with a distinctive greenish glaze on the inside. According to the 1850 U.S. Census, they used twenty cords of wood, twenty tons of clay and one thousand pounds of lead annually.

Visitors to Bridgton today are probably surprised to learn that it was once a bustling industrial center, with at least ten power sites along Stevens Brook, which winds its way from Highland Lake to Long Lake. Indeed, it is these water power sites that made manufacturing enterprises in smaller towns more competitive and feasible prior to the invention and widespread use of steam-powered machinery.

Details of the earliest manufacturing developments in Bridgton are unclear, but a sawmill was built at the foot of Crotched Pond, as Highland Lake was then called, in 1788. By the 1790s, William Sears, who moved to Bridgton from Beverly, Massachusetts, in 1789, was operating the sawmill along with a gristmill. In the early days, it was difficult to move logs through town, from Highland Lake to Long Lake and markets to the south. Joseph Walker supplied the solution with a series of sluices, called the Walker log slip, which carried the wood around the dams and falls. The Walker family built on this to establish a substantial industrial enterprise.

The tanning industry, which converted raw animal hides to useful leather, was important in the Lakes Region from an early date. John Robinson moved to Windham around 1765 and established a small tanning business, and numerous tanneries operated throughout much of the nineteenth century. Leather was necessary for shoes, of course, and the sale of the hides created another product for local farmers to sell. As in most economic relationships at the time, barter played a big role, with farmers often receiving tanned leather in return for several hides that the tanner would retain to process and sell as finished leather. Perhaps just as important for local farmers, tanning also created a market for hemlock bark, which was used in the process, and there are accounts of many wagons full of bark lining up outside local tanneries.

There were several tanneries in Bridgton, but the largest one was located by the bridge across Stevens Brook on Main Street, known, logically enough, as Tannery Bridge. The first tannery here, now (in 2013) the location of the Magic Lantern Movie Theatre on Main Street, was built in 1836 by Rufus Gibbs, one of Bridgton's leading businessmen. The tannery was a prosperous business for years, processing up to ten thousand hides in a year, employing fifty men and using ten thousand cords of bark, despite two fires, one in 1855 and one in 1893.

Industrial fires can be particularly spectacular and devastating and were all the more so with the limited firefighting equipment available during the nineteenth century. William C. Holden, writing in *The Story and History of Casco, Maine* (1941), described the huge blaze that destroyed the tannery complex in Casco:

> *One dark evening in the late '70s, fire started in the tannery building proper, making it impossible to get water from the mill pond or the brook. And all efforts to extinguish the fire were unavailing, Casco beheld the most terrible conflagration in her history. The buildings themselves were fuel for a fierce*

The tannery in Bridgton, now the site of the Magic Lantern Theatre. *Courtesy Bridgton Historical Society.*

> *blaze, but when the heat ignited the immense piles of bark, dry as tinder, it was a veritable inferno.*
>
> *The writer, hanging to his mother's hand, went across the field and crouched behind the bark piles on the South side of the road to shield himself from the heat, watching the progress of the fire. Most of the women and children of the village were there, while the men fought desperately, though with little success, to keep the flames from spreading. Those who had taken refuge behind the bark piles had to run, even as far as Frank Curtis' field. Both the starch factory and tannery were total losses. Neither was rebuilt for many years and no attempt was made to use the water power.*

Rufus Gibbs (1800–1892), one of the major property owners in Bridgton, actually got his start working in a tannery in South Bridgton that belonged to Major Thomas Perley. He and John Hall built the Cumberland Mill, a textile mill, later known as the Little Gibbs Mill, at the foot of Highland Lake. A year later, Hall sold his interest to Gibbs. The mill produced up to 250 wool blankets per day and produced blankets for the U.S. government during the

Civil War. Gibbs also operated a sawmill and shingle mill at these power sites, which are where the town beach and Shorey Park are today.

By the latter part of the nineteenth century, there were at least ten different power sites in Bridgton, with a tannery; a corn canning plant; and factories turning out lumber, furniture, building materials and other finished wood products, textiles, shoes and machinery. Before steam engines came into general use, the efficient use of water power was critical. The Perry Turbine, a significant advance in this technology, was actually invented in Bridgton. Named for William Fessenden Perry, who presumably invented the device, "The Perry Turbine Water Wheel" was a simple, rugged design that greatly increased the efficiency of water-powered machinery.

This all took place in the lower village, where, in 1861, William Perry and George Taylor purchased a large tract of land on both sides of Stevens Brook. They built an iron foundry and machine shop. The Forest Mills Company was organized after Taylor's death in 1878. It was a sprawling industrial facility, but some details of its operations remain unclear to this day, and with the exception of some of the abutments and foundations, no physical trace of it remains. In 1887, the iron foundry and machine shop became the Bridgton Machine Company, owned by Forest Mills. In addition to the

The sprawling Forest Mills complex in Bridgton. *Courtesy Bridgton Historical Society.*

The interior of the Pondicherry Woolen Mill, Bridgton, in the early twentieth century. *Courtesy Bridgton Historical Society.*

turbines, the company made shingle machines and other manufacturing parts and equipment.

The Pondicherry Woolen Mill, which was a huge building at the corner of Portland Road and Lower Main Street, was built in 1865 by Frederick J. Littlefield and his two brothers-in-law, Alvin Davis and Frederick Storer. Rufus Gibbs took over the company in 1873, adding it to the Gibbs Mill at the other end of Main Street. According to the 1904 *Bridgton Town Register*, the company had 225 employees, with a total monthly payroll of $7,000. The mill had adapted to changing times and added demand, building a one-hundred-foot chimney and switching to coal-fired power around 1900. Several different companies operated in the Pondicherry Mill through the first half of the twentieth century, and textile production continued with the Bridgton Knitting Mill on Portland Street (Route 302), which operated from 1962 until 1998.

The Bridgton Knitting Mill was owned by Malden Mills, Inc, a textile manufacturer in Malden, Massachusetts. In 1979, the company started making Polarfleece, a 100 percent polyester product capable of drawing moisture away from the body while providing warmth. Polartec, the name that the company trademarked for the product in 1991, was the fabric of choice for high-performance athletic and aerobic apparel. Among Malden's first major customers was Patagonia, which produced outerwear for mountain climbers and hikers. But Malden Mills is best known for the devastating fire in December 1995 that destroyed much of its main factory in Massachusetts and injured thirty-three employees. CEO Aaron Feurstein received widespread praise for his decision to rebuild and not only assured workers of their jobs but also paid full salaries to those unable to work during reconstruction. During this period, the mill in Bridgton continued to operate. Unfortunately, once the new mill in Massachusetts was up and running, the Bridgton mill was shut down. Shortly afterward, the Pleasant Mountain Moc Division of Sebago, Inc, which was operating a mill on Portland Street at the time, also closed. The two closures cost the area hundreds of jobs.

Bridgton also had a large corn canning plant, built in 1865 by J. Winslow Jones Corn Packing Company at the corner of Main and Elm Street. In 1889, it moved to a new site on Depot Street, which was closer to the railroad. In 1902, the Burnham and Morrill Company bought the plant, which provided work for about one hundred people and brought in $350,000 per year. Burnham and Morrill also operated a "corn shop," as the packing operations were called, in Casco. The first such operation in that town was opened by the Portland Packing Company in 1869, and there were similar packing companies at Webb's Mills and in the towns of South Windham, Raymond and Hiram. These factories employed large numbers of people on a seasonal basis, and in the early days, everything was done by hand, even making the cans, a process that kept a few men employed year-round. The ears were husked by hand and the kernels cut from the cobs with a special knife. The shop in Raymond is said to have employed 150 people, and photographs of this shop, like the shop in Bridgton, show a veritable throng of employees posing outside the building. However, with time, the processes became automated, employing fewer people and driving smaller companies out of the business. While a few textile mills and a handful of somewhat specialized manufacturing concerns continued to operate into the latter part of the twentieth century and, in some cases, beyond, this seems to embody the fate of industry in the Lakes Region.

Chapter 4

TIES THAT BIND

The Life of a Settled Society

IMPACT OF THE CIVIL WAR

By the midpoint of the nineteenth century, the identities of the communities that comprise the Sebago Lakes Region had been settled and political boundaries defined. The combined population of the towns that have been included in our informal definition of the region had been rising steadily throughout the century and stood at just a bit more than 17,500. But that figure was to fall steadily, and it would not be for another century or so that it would return to that level. This certainly paints a picture of declining influence for the region, particularly when one considers the continued population growth of the country as a whole during the entire period. The Lakes Region suffers even in comparison with the population of Maine, which grew at a considerably slower rate than did the United States as a whole.

The Civil War is often pointed to as a reason for this decline in rural northern New England during the second half of the nineteenth century. Indeed, there are many stories of men who enlisted and survived the ordeal but did not return home to stay, opting instead to move west, where new, fertile farmland was opening up. There has also been a tendency to conclude that it was "the best and the brightest" who left New England to seek their fortune in the wide open spaces of the West, but, as Hal Barron pointed out in his 1984 book, *Those Who Stayed Behind: Rural Society in Nineteenth-Century New England*, this is not the whole story. There were other demographic influences at work as well. Property ownership was key to economic success. This was particularly true for farmers, who made their living directly from the land. In the Lakes Region, as in much of northern New England, there was simply not enough land to go around, and much of the land that was available was composed of thin, rocky soil, which had lost much of what little fertility it might have had to begin with. Additionally, the hilly terrain that characterizes so much of the Sebago Lakes Region was unsuitable for the highly efficient mechanized agriculture that was developing in the plains states. Frequently, whatever local opportunity was available fell to the youngest son, who was likely to be reaching adulthood at about the time his father was reaching the age at which he could no longer actively manage the farm.

Even so, the Civil War marked a turning point in the nation's history that affected the Lakes Region every bit as much as anywhere else. The strong emotions brought on by the conflict surely affected those who lived through it. Edwin Peabody Fitch, who was born in 1840 and grew up in South Bridgton in the Bridgton Historical Society's "Narramissic," recalls an incident when one of the town's leading citizens, Nathaniel Littlefield, led what amounted to a mob to break up an abolitionist meeting. Fitch was deeply involved in the politics of the day, despite his young age. In his memoirs, which were published as *Ninety Years of Living,* he also describes the hotly-contested presidential elections of the 1850s, replete with stories of voters willing to sell their vote to the highest bidder, and his own actions in keeping an uncertain voter busy in a remote corner of the Fitch's farm all day, so that he would not have a chance to get to the polling place.

He read with interest about the debates between Stephen Douglas and Abraham Lincoln and concluded that "the long-legged, uncouth railsplitter had a tremendous mind and used it most effectively." Four years later, when Lincoln ran for president, Edwin took part in the Republicans' "Wide Awake" clubs. He traveled as far as eighteen miles to show his loyalty to the party, "strutting around with a few hundred men and boys, waving flaming torches and thinking we were terrifying the enemy by force of numbers and by our fierce looks." He commented that, after Lincoln was elected, "the excitement, instead of subsiding, grew more intense." The diary he kept as a soldier in the Civil War (published as part of *Ninety Years of Living)* describes just how exciting this was. He was captured by Rebel troops after twisting his ankle during a strategic retreat. He lost over sixty pounds during his captivity and was eventually released in a prisoner exchange. He made his way home and married his childhood sweetheart. They moved to Wisconsin and ultimately ended up in California.

Governor Henry B. Cleaves dedicates the Soldier's Monument in Bridgton in 1910. *Courtesy Bridgton Historical Society.*

Edwin Peabody Fitch was just one of the two hundred men from Bridgton who enlisted and served in the Civil War. A memorial at the top of Main Hill commemorates those Bridgton men who served in the Civil War, thirty-six of whom died during the conflict. The thirty-six-foot-tall monument consists of a figure of a soldier, with four panels on the base: "In Honor of the Living: In Grateful Memory of the Dead. To Bridgton's Sons who defended the Union, 1861–1865. They Strove That The Nation Might Live: That Government Of the People, By The People, For The People, Should Not Perish. One Country, One Destiny, One Flag." A crowd of three thousand turned out on July 21, 1910, for the monument's dedication ceremony, which featured Bridgton native Henry B. Cleaves, who was governor of Maine from 1892 to 1896 and was himself a veteran of the Civil War.

Another Civil War veteran, Major Henry Shorey, is surely one of the key figures in the history of the Lakes Region. Originally from Bath, Maine, he enlisted in the Fifteenth Maine Regiment in 1861. He moved to Bridgton after the war and founded the *Bridgton News* in 1870. His son, Henry A.

(Harry) Shorey, took over the newspaper in 1923, and his grandson Henry A. Shorey III became the publisher in 1952. When he became the Bridgton postmaster in 1956, his wife, Eula Shorey, took over as managing editor. An award-winning journalist, she somehow also found time to contribute actively to most of Bridgton's civic organizations and to raise a family. By the time she passed away at the age of ninety-seven in 2011, Stephen, Henry and Eula's son, had taken over at the *Bridgton News*, which has been arguably the single-most important source of information in and about the Sebago Lakes Region for nearly a century and a half. In 2012, the newspaper was sold to editor Wayne Rivet and his wife, Susan, ending 141 years of Shorey family ownership.

EDUCATION IN THE LAKES REGION

The survival of this newspaper for so long is, in part, testament to a long tradition of literacy and respect for the value of education. It is often unclear exactly when schools were first established in any given town, but as was the case throughout New England, the towns in the Sebago Lakes Region established a system of neighborhood primary schools, with a number of separate districts in each town, at an early date. In Bridgton, for example, the first town meeting held after the town's incorporation in 1794 voted to raise money for a school system.

Every neighborhood had its schoolhouse, with students of all ages seated in one room. This made the teacher's job a particularly challenging one, since she or he had to deal with students ranging from the first to the eighth grades at the same time. Typically, the school year was divided into two terms, a summer term and a winter term, each six to ten weeks long; later this was often expanded to three terms. Use of one-room schoolhouses continued into the twentieth century, with a few hanging on until the 1930s.

The school buildings themselves were typically one-story structures, with their gable end facing the road. Some survive today, often as private residences. There were usually two doors in front, one for girls and one for boys. Each of these doors opened into a vestibule where the students hung their coats and hats before entering the single classroom. The pupils' desks faced the teacher's desk and blackboards, which often were not actually slate, but plaster walls painted black. The only source of heat was a wood stove, and typically, there were two outhouses to the rear of the school, one for

An early photo of Bridgton Academy in North Bridgton. *Courtesy Bridgton Historical Society.*

girls and one for boys. These one-room schoolhouses often provided the only educational experience for the area's children.

However, there was interest in providing education beyond this level from the early years of settlement. In 1808, Samuel Andrews of North Bridgton, Enoch Perley of South Bridgton and Dr. Samuel Farnsworth of the center village each contributed $500 to build an academy to provide such an education, and a total of $5,000 was raised. However, the decision on where to locate the school was not an easy one, and the community became embroiled in a bitter dispute. The various factions eventually found common ground and settled on North Bridgton as the proper site. Bridgton Academy was coeducational from the start, with its first catalog listing "males" and "ladies." It served many of the educational needs of Bridgton and the surrounding towns throughout the nineteenth century and beyond, even after the establishment of public high schools, which was encouraged by state legislation in the 1870s. Bridgton Academy has been able to survive into the twenty-first century by finding a unique niche, as the nation's only all-male, strictly post-secondary school, helping to better prepare young men for college. Nearby Fryeburg Academy was incorporated in 1792 and also continues today as a college preparatory school serving students from local communities and around the world.

Bridgton High School was established in 1872, after the state passed a law providing matching funds to cover students' tuition for any town that

Bridgton High School, built in 1872. The fire station, now the headquarters of the Bridgton Historical Society, is on the right. *Courtesy Bridgton Historical Society.*

constructed a suitable building. The building became the elementary school in 1949, when a new high school was built nearby on Depot Street. The high school was replaced by Lake Region High School in 1969. It is part of SAD 61, which also includes Casco, Naples and Sebago, in addition to Bridgton. The original Bridgton High School building is now gone. After unsuccessful efforts to find alternative uses, it was torn down in 1990.

A graduate of Bridgton Academy, Joseph Fitch Potter of Sebago became a doctor and moved to Cincinnati, Ohio. He bequeathed a trust fund to the town of Sebago to be used to maintain an academy, with free tuition for students from the town. Potter Academy opened in 1895, a major event for Sebago. Handbills invited one and all to attend the dedication ceremonies on September 23, promising "Music, Speaking, and Reading." The guest speaker was no less a personage than the state superintendent of schools, and the entertainment was provided by the Hatch and Skillin Concert Company of Portland. The academy closed in 1967, and the building later burned.

In Windham, the Friends (Quakers) established an academy very early, although it did not last. Several men, including William Warren, Josiah Webb, Edwin Elder and Joseph W. Knight, taught what we would term high school classes, but the town did not establish a public high school until 1893, when it was mandated by state law.

Architect's rendering of Lake Region High School, Naples, which opened in 1969. *Courtesy Bridgton Historical Society.*

The towns of the Lakes Region developed public libraries in the late nineteenth and early twentieth centuries, often as an outgrowth of earlier reading groups. They were frequently kept in individual homes or businesses before obtaining their own building. The story of the Caswell Public Library in Harrison exemplifies the evolution of many Maine small-town public libraries. The Village Library Association started collecting books in the nineteenth century, housing approximately two hundred of them in an attorney's office. The "Reform Club" established a library in 1875 for its members and others, although a fee was charged for its use. Apparently interest in this library diminished, and Bridgton Academy, which is located very close to the Harrison line, took over the Village Library Association's collection. In 1903, the Wyonegonic Club was formed to retrieve the books from both of these collections and opened a library in 1905. The next year, the Harrison Public Library Association was incorporated. A huge fire destroyed the building in 1907, but the collection was saved, and in 1908, Daniel Caswell donated money to construct an attractive stone building that housed the library for the rest of the twentieth century, although it has since moved to a newer facility.

The Bridgton library was founded in 1895, acquired its own building in 1900 and moved to its permanent location in 1913, when the Dalton Homes Davis Library building was built with a bequest from Mr. Davis. Naples has had a library since 1907, and in Steep Falls (part of Standish), an impressive library building opened in 1916, thanks to money left to the town by Henry Pierce, who had gone west to make his fortune in the gold rush. Sebago opened its Spaulding Memorial Library in 1925, with money from Leon Spaulding, on land donated by Harry Fitch. By the middle of the twentieth century, all the towns in the region had public libraries, or at least access to libraries in adjacent communities.

THE ARRIVAL OF SUMMER PEOPLE

Even before the railroad made it easier for travelers to visit the Lakes Region, visitors were coming to vacation here, and tourism has been an important part of the economy since the nineteenth century. Many of the earliest summer people to descend on the region seem to have been as much interested in the inland mountain locations as the lakes. By 1880, summer boardinghouses were appearing, offering the farm families who operated them an extra source of income, while their guests received the benefits of fresh air, country living and often breathtaking mountain views. It was one strategy many New England farmers adopted in order to survive and (they hoped) prosper in the face of challenges posed by a declining farm economy, a loss of population and a host of pressures and changes brought on by the urbanization and modernization that was transforming the country in the nineteenth century.

In Sebago, the first such boarding house was apparently opened by A.K.P. Ward, who was operating what was known as "Lake View House" by 1880. By 1885, seven such boardinghouses were operating in the town. The earliest and perhaps most successful of these guesthouses were mostly inland hill farms, offering a country experience of fresh air, sunshine and, frequently, spectacular views. The summer resort and tourist industry became increasingly important; by 1930, it was second only to dairying in economic importance for northern New England.

Often family or social groups would summer in the same locale. Douglas Hill in Sebago, for example, which served a somewhat more upscale clientele, attracted members of the New York medical profession. According to the *Centennial History of Sebago,* at least three doctors from Brooklyn built houses here in the 1890s (one of which was sold to another New York doctor on the first one's death). Additionally, the Pike farm, located nearby, was restored by a woman from Brooklyn; it is probable that she had some connection to these other New Yorkers.

An old postcard showing vacationers enjoying the beach at North Sebago, circa 1900. *Collection of the author.*

Other summer visitors stayed at inns and sometimes in lakeshore tents, and around 1900, relatively modest, middle-class cottages began to appear along shorefronts. Some places—Ingalls Grove in Bridgton, for example—saw the tents replaced by rustic cabins. Owen Ingalls leased land on the eastern shore of Highland Lake in Bridgton to families who set up tents to live in for their lakeside holiday. Some of them signed one-hundred-year leases and built their own cottages. Later generations of these families were finally able to buy the land, thanks to Andrew Sanborn, Ingalls's grandson, who inherited the leases.

The Birches, a small development on the west shore of Highland Lake, was used by Bridgton residents who wanted a place on the water but did not want, or need, to leave town. On Sebago Lake, a project called "Sebago Beach Park" in East Sebago was laid out as a grid of fifty-nine lots, mostly fifty by one hundred feet, squeezed into less than half a mile of lake frontage, with even more lots on the inland side of the road. The leisure class was expanding.

There were also, of course, substantial hotels serving a more upscale clientele. The Bridgton House and the Cumberland Hotel were two major hotels in Bridgton, and for several decades during the latter half of the nineteenth century, there was even a hotel on top of Pleasant Mountain.

Ingalls Grove in Bridgton, a development of cottages on Highland Lake that began as a campground. *Courtesy Bridgton Historical Society.*

A view of "The Birches," a development of lakeside cottages owned primarily by Bridgton residents on Highland Lake in Bridgton. *Courtesy Bridgton Historical Society.*

Known as the Pleasant Mountain House, it was built in June 1850. Visitors could climb the mountain or take a horse-drawn carriage to the summit. The original hotel, which included a bowling alley, burned in 1860, but Charles E. Gibbs replaced it with a twenty-six-room hotel in 1873. Over

The Pleasant Mountain House hotel, built atop Pleasant Mountain in 1850. *Courtesy Bridgton Historical Society.*

three hundred people came to the grand opening on the Fourth of July that year. A band from Boston was hired to play for the occasion. In spite of the spectacular view, it does not appear to have prospered, and it was closed for much of the 1880s and 1890s. It was renovated and reopened in 1901, but even equipped with the modern amenity of a telephone, it was unprofitable. Plagued by vandalism, it was torn down a few years later, and the lumber was used for buildings on a farm in nearby East Fryeburg.

Advancements in transportation continued to make the region more accessible to urbanites, and the region was served by a full range of transportation options, including stagecoach lines, trains, steamboats and eventually, of course, automobiles. The major land routes from Portland to the interior of New Hampshire and Vermont seem to have passed up the eastern shore of the lake, through Windham, Raymond, Casco and Naples, where runs present-day Route 302.

An old postcard of the steamboat and stagecoach at Plummer's Landing in Bridgton, circa 1900. *Courtesy Bridgton Historical Society.*

Stagecoach lines served the region, often in conjunction with a steamboat or railroads. The stagecoach, which we generally associate with the "Wild West," was a widespread, if uncomfortable, means of transportation throughout the country. By 1815, a regularly scheduled stage line connected Bridgton to Norway to the north and Portland to the south, and various stage lines continued to serve the Sebago Lakes Region. By 1885, one such line ran from Steep Falls on the Maine Central Railroad, which was then the Portland and Ogdensburg, to the town of Sebago. As late as the early decades of the twentieth century, stagecoach lines were often used in conjunction with train or passenger vessels to take travelers to their final destination.

Steamships first appeared on the waters of Sebago around 1840, when the Sebago and Long Lake Steamship Company was established for transporting freight. In 1847, a newly formed company, the Sebago and Long Pond Steam Navigation Company, launched the *Fawn*, a side-wheeler that was built in North Bridgton for a cost of $8,000. It was the first passenger steamship on the lakes, with a schedule that met the stage to Portland at Standish.

According to the *Bicentennial History of Harrison, Maine, 1905–2005*, compiled by the Harrison Historical Society, *Fawn* was exceedingly top-heavy, with an engine and boiler that were far too large for it, and according to a local writer, when it went through the Songo River from Brandy Pond to Sebago, famous for its twists and turns, "the passengers literally worked their passage…they being used as ballast to keep her evenly balanced by dint

A very crowded steamboat going through the locks, probably circa 1880. From a stereoview. *Courtesy Bridgton Historical Society.*

of going from one side to the other as she went round the sharp curves." In 1857, the engine and boiler were sold to a group starting a steamship service on Moosehead Lake.

Later, the side-wheelers *Oriental*, *Sebago* and *Mount Pleasant* provided service on the lakes. The *Sebago* burned at the Bridgton landing in 1873 and was replaced with the screw-propelled *Hawthorne*, which operated for thirty-five years. The *Goodridge*, *Worrambus*, *Songo*, *Sokokis*, *Hiawatha*, *Minnehaha* and *Bay of Naples* all provided service on the lakes for many years. The *Bay of Naples* has an interesting story, having been built in Racine, Wisconsin, in 1906,

Cover of a brochure advertising the Songo River Steamship Line. *Courtesy Bridgton Historical Society.*

The Naples Causeway, showing the Bay of Naples Inn in the background, from an old postcard. *Collection of the author.*

where it was disassembled before being shipped to Naples for reassembly. In 1931, both the *Bay of Naples* and the *Goodridge* burned, bringing an end to regularly scheduled daily service. In the twenty-first century, the *Songo River Queen II,* a replica of a paddle-wheel steamboat, continued to provide tourist excursions. Because of the replacement of the swing bridge on the Naples Causeway with a fixed bridge, it took its last voyage into Brandy Pond and down the Songo River locks on September 17, 2011.

The replacement of this bridge means that large vessels will no longer be able to complete the trip from Sebago Lake to Long Lake, making it impossible to replicate an extended excursion that was possible in the nineteenth century. Travelers back then could take the train from Portland, or even Boston, to Sebago Lake Station at the foot of Sebago Lake in Standish. There they could board a steamboat that would take them through the Songo Locks into Long Lake and all the way to Harrison. They could return to Standish on the steamboats or connect with the narrow-gauge railroad in Bridgton, changing in Hiram for the return trip to the "big city." Such newfound easy access to previously remote rural regions created a whole new relationship between city people and the Sebago Lakes Region, a relationship that was to have a profound effect on the area in the twentieth century.

SUMMER CAMPS

Such advances in transportation also opened up the area for another whole set of visitors: youngsters who came to attend camp. Summer camps for children first appeared in the United States in the 1880s. Late Victorian ideals stressed the moral and physical value of an experience in the country, where, according to the theory, nature and fresh air could counteract the corrupting influence of urban life. The earliest camps were in the mountains and lakes regions in New Hampshire and catered to the wealthy elite. However, the 1890s saw a proliferation of summer camps that served a wider clientele. While more and more private camps catered to middle-class children, religious and social welfare organizations provided camping experiences to poor children from what we would now term the inner city.

The Sebago Lakes Region, as a rural area with an abundance of lakes, located within a few hours of Boston by train, attracted a number of camp operators. As Porter Sargent put it in his *Handbook of Summer Camps, 1925:*

> *Although the first camps for boys and girls were established elsewhere, the attractions of the Maine woods and lakes early brought pioneer camps to the regions about Sebago Lake and Long Lake. The numerous lakes and the great extent of woodland, as well as the proximity to the White Mountains on the one hand and salt water on the other, have resulted in a great development of summer camps in Maine.*

In 1909, Charlotte Gulick, wife of Dr. Luther Gulick, established a camp known as Sebago Wohelo in Casco. This camp actually had its origins in a family camp established in 1888 on the Thames River in Connecticut. Mrs. Gulick's system later formed the basis of the Camp Fire Girls organization, which was founded in 1910, with the help of Mrs. Charles Farnsworth in Thetford, Vermont, along with the Gulicks and their work in Casco. The name "Wohelo," which is made up of the first two letters of the words work, health and love, was taken as the watchword of the Camp Fire Girls. By 1925, there were actually two local camps: Sebago Wohelo for girls ages thirteen to eighteen and Little Wohelo for younger girls. They were known collectively as the Luther Gulick Camps. Porter Sargent attributes the success of these camps to the "magnetic personality of the founders. Mrs. Gulick, although a grandmother, had that rare spontaneous enthusiasm which develops a similar enthusiasm in the girls and inspires them to creative work." The camps emphasized crafts such as weaving, pottery and jewelry

Camp Fire Girls at Sebago Lake. *From the George Grantham Bain Collection, Library of Congress.*

making, although the more traditional athletic and water-related activities were not completely ignored. The national organization, which was the first nonsectarian organization for girls in the country, became co-ed in 1975 and eventually adopted its current name: Camp Fire USA.

Camp Wenonah girls (not to be confused with Camp Winona in Bridgton) headed out for an unknown excursion, probably circa 1920. From a glass plate negative. *Courtesy Bridgton Historical Society.*

But one of the earliest camps in the country for girls was Wyonegonic, a private camp established on the shores of Moose Pond in Denmark in 1902. Its companion camp, Camp Winona, also on Moose Pond but in Bridgton, was founded in 1908, making the pair the oldest brother/sister camps in the nation. Another camp for girls, Camp Al-Ky-Ris, on Sebago Lake, provided extremely comfortable, if not downright luxurious, conditions for its campers and staff. It boasted that two hundred-acre farms provided fresh country food, "supplemented by the best the city markets offered." This food was served in a well-equipped dining hall. In addition, the facility included ten detached bungalows, a playhouse and theater, electric lights and "the most modern sanitation." Other camps provided a less pampered experience. For example, the director of Camp Wyonee in Harrison, Dr. Frederic H. Wilson, believed that true camping did not mean "baseball games and other athletics as much as actual camping out and cooking by the boys themselves."

There are forty-five camps identified on Sargent's 1925 map of the Long Lake and Sebago Lake Region. While all the camps seem to have provided swimming, boating, hiking and other activities, many filled a particular niche. For example, Camp Mechano in Raymond was "for the boy interested in mechanical science, who wishes to acquire a working knowledge of automobiles, motor boats, radio, advanced photography or astronomy." It was equipped with a variety of engines and a radio plant, in addition to canoes, boats and sport facilities.

Long Lake Lodge in North Bridgton, on the other hand, was strictly for tutoring older boys for college examinations in the fall. It was founded in 1902 by Edwin Victor Spooner, a French instructor at Phillips Exeter Academy. Interestingly, Bridgton Academy, also in North Bridgton, is now a strictly post-secondary school for boys, serving much the same purpose that Long Lake Lodge did.

A number of camps were affiliated with religious organizations. Some camps catered to Jewish children. Camp Chickawah in Harrison for example, was a camp for Jewish boys and stressed that the "Jewish dietary law was strictly adhered to," and Camp Tapawingo, also in Harrison, was for Jewish girls. In Bridgton, Camp Coda was for Jewish boys and Camp Woodlands was for Jewish girls, and in the twenty-first century, there are still two Jewish camps in Bridgton: JCC Maccabbi Camp Kingswood and Camp Micah.

Camp O-AT-KA was founded in East Sebago in 1906 by Reverend Ernest Joseph Dennen, an Episcopal minister from Lynn, Massachusetts. He brought twenty boys from his parish the first summer, as a reward for their achievements in a character-building program known as the "Order of Sir Galahad." At first, the boys—twenty the first year—slept in canvas tents, but a bungalow was constructed in 1907, and by 1930, the camp boasted an entire campus, with a "Great Hall," commons building and other structures. With over sixty buildings, two playing fields, five tennis courts, a covered basketball court, rifle and archery ranges and a seven-studio arts center, by 2011, it could accommodate 150 campers, representing thirty states and twelve foreign countries, at one time.

The Boy Scouts have Camp Hinds in Raymond, with over 280 acres on Panther Pond, while Camp Pondicherry in Bridgton is run by the Girl Scouts, and today there continue to be too many summer camps in the region to list them all. Some date back to the early twentieth century, while others have been founded more recently. However, there are two camps with special missions that deserve extra attention: Camp Sunshine in Casco and Seeds of Peace in Otisfield.

Camp Sunshine was founded in 1984 by Anna M. Gould and Dr. Lawrence Gould at Point Sebago Resort. It is actually a year-round facility that serves children with life-threatening illnesses and their immediate families. The program is free of charge and sees the children and their loved ones through various stages of the child's illness. The camp offers onsite medical and psychosocial support around the clock and includes bereavement groups for those families who suffer the loss of a child to an illness.

Seeds of Peace was founded in 1993 by journalist John Weallch. It is "dedicated to empowering young leaders from regions of conflict with the leadership skills required to advance reconciliation and coexistence." Each year it brings together teenagers from areas in the world experiencing intense conflicts. It started with 46 Israeli, Palestinian and Egyptian teenagers in 1993. It has since expanded to include young people from South Asia, Cyprus and the Balkans. The summer camp experience in Otisfield is actually the beginning of the program, which continues with regional activities including dialogue meetings, conferences, workshops and educational and professional opportunities, as well as an adult educators program encouraging lasting respect and empathy between two groups in conflict. By 2012, its leadership network had grown to over 4,300 young people.

ARTS AND CULTURE

The natural beauty of the Sebago Lakes Region has appealed to artists and writers from an early time. Henry Wadsworth Longfellow, who grew up in Portland, was familiar with the area through his maternal grandfather, Peleg Wadsworth, who retired to Hiram. One of his earliest poems, "The Battle of Lovewell's Pond," which he wrote as a young boy and submitted anonymously to a local newspaper, commemorated the fight between the Pequawkets and Captain John Lovewell's band in Fryeburg, described previously. On a visit later in life, Longfellow apparently took a steamboat excursion on the lakes and wrote "The Songo River," an evocative description of the meandering waterway that connects Sebago Lake and Brandy Pond, excerpted below:

Nowhere such a devious stream,
Save in history or in dream,
Winding slow through brush and brake,
Links together lake and lake.

Walled with woods or sandy shelf,
Ever doubling on itself,
Flows the stream, so still and slow,
That it hardly seems to flow…

Though thou turnest no busy mill,
And art ever calm and still,
Even thy silence seems to say
To the traveler on his way—

"Traveler, hurrying from the heat
Of the city, stay thy feet!
Rest awhile, nor longer waste
Life with inconsiderate haste!"

Nathaniel Hawthorne, a classmate of Longfellow's at Bowdoin College, also has connections to the Lakes Region. His father, a sea captain, died in Surinam when Nathaniel was just four years old. A few years later, when he was nine, his mother's brother built a house for her in Raymond. It is not clear just how much time he spent here, but later writings and an early diary that he kept at the suggestion of his uncle, Richard Manning, demonstrate that the experiences made a strong impression on him. His favorite spot was a large flat rock where Dingley Brook flows into Thomas Pond. Shortly before his death in 1864, he wrote, "I lived in Maine like a bird of the air, so perfect was the freedom I enjoyed." The interior of the Hawthorne House was converted for use as a church and eventually fell into disrepair. In 1922, it was taken over by the Hawthorne Community Association and is used for occasional social and cultural events.

The fresh air, lakes and mountain views also attracted a number of visual artists and performers to the region during the increasingly busy summer months. Frederick Bristol was a highly regarded music teacher from New York, who summered in Harrison. Many of his famous pupils followed him here. One of them was opera star Marie Sundelius, whom the *History of Harrison* describes as "one of the most beloved of the summer residents of Harrison." Another opera star, Madame Olive Fremstad, built a summer home, which she dubbed "Newandyn," on the shore of Highland Lake in Bridgton, not far from Harrison. Thus the Saco Valley Music Festival, which was held at the Bridgton Town Hall for many years in the early decades of the twentieth century, was able to avail itself of some world-class talent.

Visual artists were also attracted to the area. Charles Fox was an important if somewhat little-known early modern painter, who along with fellow artist Curtis Perry, ran a loose-knit school on Highland Ridge in Bridgton, where the two built a large, symmetrical house overlooking Highland Lake and Pleasant Mountain. Fox, who trained at the Ecole des Beaux-Arts in Paris was active

Photograph of opera star Marie Sundelius, who summered in Harrison, autographed for Eva Shorey of Bridgton. *Courtesy Bridgton Historical Society.*

from around 1880 until 1927, when he died. A Socialist who ran for governor twice, he was also a music lover, putting on concerts in his house and playing the latest phonograph records. Guy Monk, in his short book *The Story of North Bridgton, Maine*, described the two artists as a casually dressed, unlikely pair, with the tall and slender Fox contrasting with the shorter Perry. They also created an extraordinary garden by the road above their house. They had tons of rock, blasted from a ledge six miles away with a striking mix of granite and other minerals, hauled to their property. It took twelve yokes of oxen to move the large central rock, which stood eight feet high, and the garden was a well-known landmark and attraction. Sadly, the two eventually quarreled and never reconciled.

In Harrison, one summer resident, opera singer, voice coach and director Enrica Clay Dillon, made a great contribution to the artistic and cultural life of the region when she fulfilled her dream of creating an opera house to foster artistic development. She brought her students to Harrison each summer, and as the productions outgrew her porch, she built a theater. Designed by Harrison Wiseman of New York, Deertrees opened in 1936 with near-perfect acoustics, a stage that was exactly the same size as that of the Metropolitan Opera House and state-of-the-art technical equipment. No expense was spared in the construction, which cost $60,000, an extravagant amount for those days. The Adirondack-style building, which seats three hundred, was constructed of rose hemlock and featured hand-carved woodwork and light fixtures. The property was located near a natural salt lick that attracted deer, so Ms. Dillon named the snack bar "the Salt Lick Café."

Deertrees got off to an auspicious start on August 15, 1936, when it was christened with a bottle of champagne as classical actor Walter Hampden read from *Cyrano de Bergerac*. The sponsors and supporters included celebrities like Helen Hayes, Humphrey Bogart and the steel magnate Schwab family. Although 1937 was apparently a successful season, with six different productions staged on a rotating basis, the theater did not open in 1938. In an explanation published in the August 5, 1938 *Bridgton News*, Enrica Dillon wrote that the theatre was intended to be "a laboratory and experimental theatre where problems, both artistic and educational, could be worked out in perfect surroundings." But in 1939, she leased the facility to Hungarian-born theater producer Bela Blau, who operated it as a summer theater. His productions included some of the biggest stars of the day, including Ethyl Barrymore, Talullah Bankhead, Arthur Treacher, Dame Mae Whittey, Joe E. Brown and Rudy Vallee. As an aside, rumors flew locally about Vallee's wild parties, women, speedboats and nude sunbathing at his house in Lovell.

Even so, the locals apparently supported Deertrees, which had been dubbed "Maine's most enchanting theatre." At the end of the summer of 1939, the board of selectmen went to Blau and expressed their support and appreciation, promising to improve the rough gravel road that led to the theater. Community members donated time and equipment, and the next spring, there was a good solid road to the theatre.

The beautiful theater with perfect acoustics did, however, have one problem. During a heavy rainstorm, the sound on the walls and roof was deafening, and performances had to be suspended until the storm passed. Despite the occasional hiccup from such occurrences, Blau put together another successful season in 1940. Unfortunately, he died of a heart attack in October of that year. Nearly fifty years after his death, the theater brought back Blau's practice of bringing recent New York plays to Harrison, with their complete casts, and created "The Friends of Bela Blau" to designate subscribers to this series.

After Blau's passing, Ms. Dillon formed the Deertrees Opera Company, which operated into 1942. World War II intervened, and the theater remained closed until 1946, when it reopened for a "Summer Festival of Opera and Drama." Again an untimely death interrupted the theater's life; this time it was the founder herself, Enrica Clay Dillon, at the age of seventy-two. For the next three decades or so, the theater went through several ownerships. In 1965, Mrs. Aya Sholley, who had acquired the property in 1956, gave it to her alma mater, Emerson College. For several years, Emerson students, under the supervision of their instructors, received academic credit for producing professional-quality plays. However, business was slow, the college was losing money on the property and the facilities were in need of repair. In 1969, the college sold it to twenty-one-year-old David Maturi, a former student who had worked at the theater. He and Alfred Corono founded the Coventry Center for the Performing Arts, presenting light comedy and musical shows and working with local restaurants to create dinner and theater specials. However, the Coventry Center was no more able to turn a profit than Emerson College, and in 1974, the property was again sold, this time to Mr. and Mrs. Donald Ritter, who produced opera and experimental theater.

By 1979, it was clear that this was not a winning combination at the box office. The theater closed and was taken over by porcupines, and the town of Harrison gained title to the property in lieu of taxes. The plan was to burn it as an exercise for the fire department. Fortunately, Dr. Allan Mills, a biochemist who had played bit parts at Deertrees in his youth, checked out the situation and confirmed that the building was salvageable. He brought together a group of concerned citizens and formed the Deertrees Foundation to save the historic building and develop programs to use it. The first performances were held on the front porch, because the building itself was unsafe. By the early 1990s, the interior restoration had progressed enough to allow use of the original stage. In 1999, the town turned over the title to the property to the Deertrees Foundation, which funds operations and ongoing restoration through box office receipts and annual fundraising campaigns. Listed in the National Register of Historic Places, Deertrees Theatre is a nonprofit performing arts center. In 2011, Deertrees was operating from June to September and offered a wide variety of performances, including standup comedy, plays and music. It is home to the Deertrees Theatre Festival, the Sebago-Long Lake Music Festival, the Deertrees Children's Wednesday Series, the BackStage Art Gallery and the Salt Lick Café.

Chapter 5

INTO THE MODERN WORLD

Twentieth-Century Transformations

At the turn of the twentieth century, the United States was still in the horse and buggy age, but in just a few decades, the widespread use of automobiles transformed the landscape and the way Americans lived their lives. The automobile made the Sebago Lakes Region even more accessible to tourists and summer people. It also made it more accessible to nearby urban areas, and by the end of the century, although the region could not be classified as truly suburban, more and more of its residents commuted to jobs in greater Portland or the Lewiston-Auburn area.

U.S. Route 302, which runs up the eastern side of Sebago Lake, is the primary transportation corridor. It follows a route that was established as a stagecoach road from Portland to Bridgton around 1800 and was historically an overland route from New Hampshire and Vermont to the coast. The easternmost section of it roughly parallels much of the early water route from Sebago Lake, through the Presumpscot River to Portland. Starting at the state line in Fryeburg, Route 302 crosses the Saco River and Moose Pond and then runs parallel to Long Lake, across the causeway in Naples. It runs east of Sebago Lake, crossing the Crooked River in Casco and the Pleasant River in Windham before heading into Portland. Particularly in North Windham, this route has seen extensive commercial "strip" development, with shopping centers, malls, fast food chains, big box stores and all the other embodiments of suburban sprawl. The major arteries on the western side of the lake, Routes 114 and 113, which connect through Gorham to Route 302 in Naples and Fryeburg respectively, have seen less concentrated commercial development.

As discussed in Chapter One, in the early years of white settlement, travel by land was extremely difficult, and although improvements were made, it remained so, at least by our current standards, into the twentieth century. In the winter, roads were kept open using huge wooden rollers, twelve feet wide and five feet high, which were drawn by teams of four or six horses, to pack down the snow. By the 1920s, towns had to start plowing roads in winter, although many dirt roads remained. In Sebago in the 1920s and 1930s, the timing of spring school vacation was determined by the condition of the Folly Road: vacation was declared when wagon wheels sank halfway into the mud.

Of course, the improvement in the quality of roads in the first few decades of the twentieth century was brought about by the rapid spread of the automobile. Today, we might assume that there would be little controversy surrounding the issue. However, around the turn of the twentieth century, as Richard W. Judd points out in his article "Good Roads for Whom?" in the June 2008 issue of *Maine History*, this was a contentious proposition. Farmers wanted a system that would simply link them to local markets and rail lines, while urban business interests and statewide agencies seeking to encourage tourism pushed for a system of "trunk lines" that would support automobile traffic from one end of the state to the other. Furthermore, road maintenance and improvement had always been handled by town government, and the proposals by those advocating the "trunk line" approach would move the administration to state agencies and require additional state taxes. A series of legislative compromises were passed during the first two decades of the twentieth century, including, in 1911, the adoption of an annual tax on automobiles, the proceeds from which were dedicated to maintaining the state roads. The road from Fryeburg to Bridgton (now Route 302), which is one of the state's two major southern gateways, was completed in 1914, making it one of the first state road projects to be completed. The expansion of the state highway system was boosted by the Federal Aid Highway Act of 1916, which made matching funds available. Local pressure also produced improved roads: for example, the first paved road came to Harrison in 1919, when, at the request of several townspeople (who contributed $245 towards the project), Main and Front Streets were covered with 3,900 gallons of Pontar, which was shipped from the E.I. Dupont Co., perhaps somewhat ironically, on the Bridgton and Saco River Railroad.

One of the distinctive sections of Route 302 is the Naples Causeway, separating Brandy Pond from Long Lake. The Bay of Naples Inn, a 102-room hotel designed by Charles Goodridge, opened in 1899. Although the

Construction of the Moose Pond Causeway on Route 302, Bridgton, 1923–1924. *Courtesy Bridgton Historical Society.*

Some of the boulders from nearby farms used in the construction of the Moose Pond Causeway. *Courtesy Bridgton Historical Society.*

inn closed in 1951 and was torn down in the 1960s, the causeway retains its distinctive personality, with restaurants, boat rides and other attractions lining the highway. During the summer months, the crowds and traffic attest to its popularity. Nearby, Sebago Lake State Park, one of the state's five original state parks, opened in 1938 on the northern shore of Sebago Lake, at the mouth of the Songo River. The park provides a wide variety of recreational opportunities, with beaches, a 250-site campground, extensive woodlands and a variety of wildlife habitats.

To the west, still on Route 302, the Moose Pond Causeway on the other side of Bridgton provides a spectacular view of Pleasant Mountain and its ski area, now known as Shawnee Peak. This is the longest continually operating ski area in Maine. On January 23, 1938, more than five hundred skiers turned out to try the state's first rope tow on a trail cut the year before by members of the Civilian Conservation Corps (CCC) and students from Bridgton Academy. The area also saw the first T-bar in the state of Maine in 1953, and two years later, a 4,300-foot chairlift was installed, also the first in Maine. In 1988, the Shawnee Group bought the operation, changed the name to "Shawnee Peak" and installed lights for night skiing. Kennebunk

The Civilian Conservation Corps camp in Bridgton (later the site of the Bridgton Hospital). *Courtesy Bridgton Historical Society.*

businessman Chet Homer bought the business in 1994 and has continued to upgrade the facility. The original sixteen- by twenty-two-foot shelter of 1938 has been replaced by a large, fully equipped base lodge and trailside condos, and night skiing is one of the area's major attractions. Just forty-five miles from Portland, it remains an accessible, family-friendly attraction.

But of course, even in the twenty-first century, the region does not exist solely for the amusement of tourists and people "from away." Like all of the country, Sebago Lakes Region residents have taken part in the nation's wars, both in combat roles and on the home front. The specific contributions of local service men and women are too numerous to elaborate in a brief work such as this, but many details can be found in the various individual town histories that have been published and at local historical societies and veterans' organizations.

During World War II, towns in the Lakes Region, like those elsewhere, organized civil defense teams to spot enemy aircraft and prepare for possible air raids. Tin cans and aluminum foil were collected to produce more military equipment. The country was mobilized to support the war effort; "Rosie the Riveter" symbolized the millions of women who went to work in industrial jobs that were traditionally given to males. Workers from the Lakes Region commuted daily to the shipyards in South Portland, which ran twenty-four

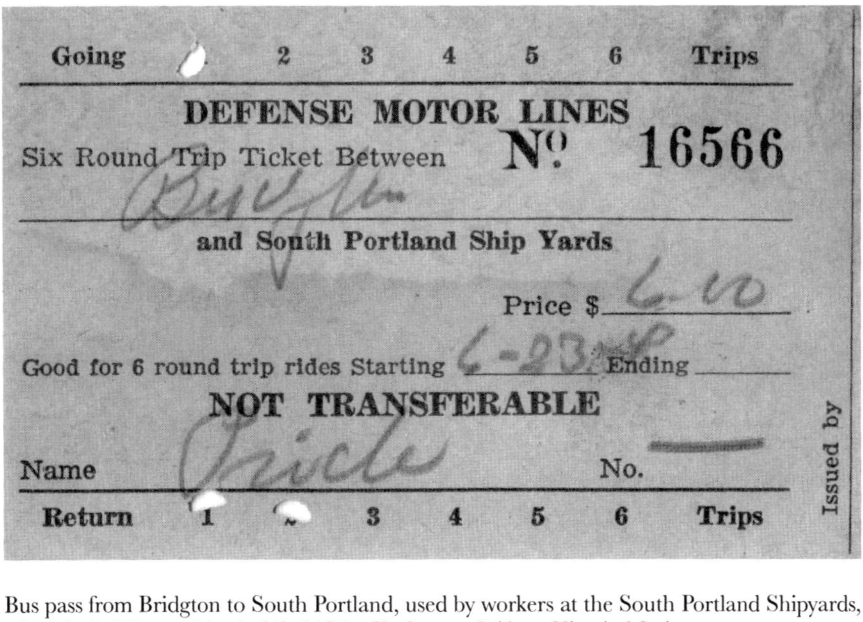

Bus pass from Bridgton to South Portland, used by workers at the South Portland Shipyards, which built Liberty ships in World War II. *Courtesy Bridgton Historical Society.*

hours per day producing Liberty ships, the workhorse of the merchant marine, which transported troops and equipment to the European and Asian theaters. There was even a bus line that ran from Bridgton to the shipyards.

The Bridgton Canning Center, one of fifty statewide, canned produce from local victory gardens. Two paid staff persons supervised volunteer workers. Gardeners who brought in their produce agreed to donate one out of every five cans for community welfare programs, disaster relief or school lunches, although many donated all of what they brought in. Other volunteers knitted socks, blankets and other items, following instructions distributed by the Red Cross.

The health care needs of Lakes Region residents were met in part by the establishment of a hospital in Bridgton. Dr. Edward Abbott spearheaded fundraising efforts in 1917, and a few years later, the Northern Cumberland Memorial Hospital opened in a large house on Main Hill in Bridgton. Although improvements were made over the course of the next several decades, by the early 1960s, enough money was raised to build an entirely new facility on South High Street by the site of the agricultural fairs that were popular during the first few decades of the twentieth century. This hospital was in turn replaced in 2002, when the name was changed to Bridgton Hospital, and it became associated with the Lewiston-based Central Maine Medical Family.

The immediate post–World War II period was not one of particular prosperity for the Lakes Region, although, as we have seen, a certain amount of industrial activity continued, and a seemingly never-ending and increasingly large stream of visitors swelled the population each year. The 1960s saw the consolidation of school systems in Maine. Bridgton, Casco, Naples and Sebago united to form the Lake Region School District, and Standish joined with Buxton, Hollis and Limington. Harrison and Otisfield became part of the Oxford Hills School District, and recently, as a result of the state-mandated consolidation, Raymond and Windham joined together as RSU 14. It is difficult to assess the impact of these changes on the different communities. While elementary school children generally attend school in their own towns, middle and senior high school students are apt to travel farther each day. One can certainly argue that when a town loses its high school, it loses a piece of its identity, and the transformation from the one-room schoolhouse system at the turn of the twentieth century to the present consolidated regional model is a dramatic one.

Of course, many attitudes have changed during that period. The sixties also saw an expanded awareness of the importance of the natural environment.

That awareness has deepened with time in the Lakes Region, whose identity and economic well being depend to a large extent on its natural resources and the maintenance of a healthy environment. In 1970, Peter Lowell in Bridgton founded the Lakes Environmental Association (LEA). As its first and, as of 2013, its only executive director, he has grown the nonprofit organization into an effective force for protecting the lakes of western Maine by providing education and technical assistance and leading efforts to protect the lakes from threats such as those posed by the invasive plant milfoil.

Against the backdrop of increasing environmental awareness, in January 1986, the U.S. Department of Energy announced that the Sebago Lake Region was on its list of potential sites for a long-term high-level nuclear waste repository, better known as a dump. Local reaction was swift and overwhelmingly negative. On February 10 of that year, three thousand people packed the Lake Region High School Gymnasium to attend an informational meeting held by Department of Energy Officials. Many showed up with printed placards with the word "NO" in large blue letters. Opposition galvanized in the region, and several groups formed. The Lake Region Anti-Nuclear Waste Fund, sponsored by the Town of Casco and joined by other area towns, raised $350,000 to fight the proposal. The Lakes Environmental Association took an active role, and Citizens Against Nuclear Trash ("CANT") was formed, led by South Casco housewife Bonnie Titcomb, who later became a state senator. Tom Andrews, then a state senator from Portland who was known for championing social justice and environmental issues, also took on an active role, and he later served two terms representing the First District of Maine in the United States Congress. Bridgton resident Bob Dunning and others researched and presented technical objections, arguing that the underlying geology of the area was unsuitable for the creation of a repository that needed to last for tens of thousands of years or more. Peter Lowell argued that it was important not just to say "Not in my backyard" but also to say "Not in this kind of backyard." There was a widespread belief that the DOE had not done its homework, that its proposals were scientifically unsound and that, among other deficiencies, it did not recognize the fact that the population of the area grew exponentially in the summer. Political pressure grew against the proposal, which had designated several other candidates for regional repositories, and the entire plan was eventually scrapped. As of this writing, more than twenty-five years later, the government has still been unable to find a site that is both scientifically and politically acceptable. Some would argue that they have not even found one that is scientifically acceptable.

As was discussed in the introduction, the population of the Lakes Region more than doubled during the last few decades of the twentieth century, growing at a rate greater than both Maine's population growth and that of the nation as a whole. "The Lake Region Greenprint" is a plan that was produced through a community-driven process, undertaken by the Trust for Public Land, which articulates goals for regional land use and the maintenance of open space. It points out that the phenomenal growth rate of the late twentieth century continued into the first decade of the twenty-first century, which saw the region's population increase by 10 percent. More people in the region today are employed in service-oriented jobs, like insurance or real estate, or are in administrative, scientific, educational or health-related professions. Most businesses are small, often seasonal, family operations. Continuing the trend of the last century, much of the economy continues to be based on providing services for tourists and summer residents, with inns, restaurants, summer camps and small construction companies. The region also made gains in median household income during this decade, although much of that may be due to the many people who own second homes in the region. Lakes Region towns experience a two- to fourfold increase in population during the summer, but many year-round residents cannot afford a second home.

Even so, the vast majority of people interviewed in the Lakes Region were very satisfied with the towns they lived in and expressed attitudes that greatly valued outdoor activities and land conservation. Interestingly, the Greenprint found that, after identifying themselves with their own town, area residents were more likely to associate themselves with the Lakes Region than with greater Portland, Lewiston-Auburn or any other nearby geographical area. More than two and a half centuries after the first white men began exploring and settling "New Marblehead" and other colonial land grants, people identify with the Lakes Region's special character, whether they visit for a few days, weeks or months, or whether they call it home.

BIBLIOGRAPHY

Anderson, Hayden L. *Canals and Inland Waterways of Maine.* Portland, ME: Maine Historical Society, 1982.

Barron, Hal S. *Those Who Stayed Behind: Rural Society in Nineteenth-Century New England.* New York: Cambridge University Press, 1984.

Bicentennial Booklet Committee. *Windham Invites You.* Windham, ME: self-published, 1938.

Dole, Frederick Howard. *Sketches of the History of Windham, Maine, 1734–1935.* Westbrook, ME: Town of Windham, 1935.

Dole, Samuel Thomas. *Windham in the Past.* Auburn, ME: Merrill & Webber Co., 1916.

Dwight, Timothy. *Travels in New England and New York*, vol. II. New Haven, CT: Timothy Dwight, 1821.

Fitch, Edwin Peabody. *Ninety Years of Living, 1840–1930.* Bridgton, ME: Evangeline Fitch Moke and Bridgton Historical Society, 1997.

Hankins, Jean and David. *A Short History of Otisfield, Maine.* Otisfield, ME: Otisfield Historical Society, 1998.

Harrison Historical Society (comp.). *Bicentennial History of Harrison, Maine 1905–2000, vol. 1 History.* Harrison, ME: self-published, 2004.

Holden, William C., assisted by the Centennial Committee on History. *The Story and History of Casco Maine*. Casco, ME: Centennial Committee on History, August 1941.

Hubka, Thomas C. *Big House, Little House, Back House, Barn: The Connected Farm Buildings of New England.* Hanover, NH: University Press of New England, 1984.

Hudson, John Bradley. "Up the Canal to the Mountains," 1859. Typescript by Franklin Allen at Bridgton Historical Society, original manuscript in the collection of the Museum of Fine Arts, Boston.

Jones, Herbert G. *Sebago Lake Land Inn History, Legend, & Romance.* Freeport, ME: Bond Wheelwright Company, 1946.

Judd, Richard W. "Good Roads for Whom?: Farmers, Urban Merchants, and Road Administration in Maine, 1901-1916." *Maine History* 43, no. 4 (June 2008).

Knight, Ernest H. *Raymond Then and Now.* Raymond, ME: Raymond Woman's Club, 1978.

Meserve, Fred L. (comp.). *Centennial History of Sebago, Maine, 1826–1926.* N.p, n.d.

Monk, Guy. *The Story of North Bridgton, Maine.* Bridgton, ME: Guy Monk, 1958.

Sargent, Porter. *A Handbook of Summer Camps, 1925.* Boston: Porter Sargent, 1925.

Sears, Albert J. *The Founding of Pearsontown (Standish), Maine.* Bowie, MD: Heritage Books, Inc., 1991.

Shorey, Eula M., and Michael T. Corrigan (eds.). *Bridgton, Maine 1768–1994: An Updated Bicentennial History.* Bridgton, ME: Bridgton Historical Society, 1994.

The Trust for Public Land and Loon Echo Land Trust. *The Lake Region Greenprint: A Community Partnership* [2010]. Available at http://cloud.tpl.org/pubs/convis-me-lake-region-report.pdf.

Wilson, Deborah. *Phase 0 Archaeological Survey Report: Eel Weir Project Ferc. No. 2984,* Prepared for S.D. Warren Co., Westbrook, Maine (Boothbay Harbor, ME: 2002).

INDEX

ABOUT THE AUTHOR

Ned Allen graduated from Bowdoin College with a BA in history and earned his masters degree in New England Studies (now American and New England Studies) from the University of Southern Maine. He has worked in history museums for twenty-five years in curatorial, educational and administrative capacities. His experience includes serving as an independent museum consultant; education coordinator for the Maine Historical Society; curator and education coordinator for the Berkshire Historical Society at Herman Melville's Arrowhead; curator of Portland Harbor Museum; executive director of Bridgton Historical Society; and collections manager of Freeport Historical Society. He grew up in Schenectady, New York, where his father was a professor of history at Union College. He and his family spent summers in Maine, usually at his grandparents' summer house, a nineteenth-century farmstead in Sebago. He and his wife, Carol Colby, live in a nineteenth-century farmhouse at the end of a dirt road in Bridgton.